THE BACK HOME SERIES

SERIES TITLES

Soul of the Outdoors
Dave Greschner

From the Heart: The Story of Matrix
John Harmon

The Long Fields
Anne-Marie Oomen

Kick Out the Bottom
Erik Mortenson & Christopher Kramer

Wrong Tree: Adventures in Wildlife Biology
Jeff Wilson

At the Lake
Jim Landwehr

Body Talk
Takwa Gordon

The In-Between State
Martha Lundin

North Freedom
Carolyn Dallmann

Ohio Apertures
Robert Miltner

Water Spell

With equal parts rigor and delight, this nonfiction collection inventories the pop culture worlds that forged this lyric speaker's strength to survive a difficult time: from *Moana* to art theory, to the heroines of manga and video games. Broadwall's observations sit somewhere in the gorgeous space of daily diary, poetry, scholarly analysis, and the narrative enmeshed in the everyday. Examining the "immaculately cindered" end of a marriage, the writing is also immaculately tender. While unpacking boxes with a new love, each domestic scene becomes its own "quiet exorcism," and the previous "desert state" emerges as a powerful symbol for not just a landscape's deprivation, but also a desolate out-of-place-ness. Broadwall knows our words can still be our sense amidst senselessness, can still be "the sea" that "is there to catch me." Here is a balm, a salve, for the way observing is processing, is creating, and a reminder that the myth of healing's finality is as inscrutable as a mermaid living on dry land.

—KATIE FULLER
author of *Careful*

Catherine Broadwall's *Water Spell* is a lush memoir about the "sorrow, rage, and relief" that comes when ending a failing marriage. In a series of intelligent and poignant vignettes, the author conjures up beautiful images from diverse sources (Disney films, manga, witch lore, mythology, and fairy tale) to mine the "agony that gets called healing." Working as bibliotherapy, Broadwall's ekphrastic reflections chart her course away from her destructive "man of mist" toward a greater understanding of her own desires, a recognition which grants her a second chance at love. As her fragmentary observations seamlessly weave together, the book becomes a heartfelt map that shows us how to walk out of the desert, even when barefoot and vulnerable. Broadwall proves that such movement, though painful, can mend our emotional wounds and lead us to potent transformation. *Water Spell* is a testament to how symbolic narratives confront, embrace, and recreate our broken past, allowing us to become whole in the here and now.

—CHRISTINE BUTTERWORTH-MCDERMOTT
author of *The Spellbook of Fruit & Flowers*

Each decade, there comes a book about the dis-enchantment of a relationship as innovatively written as it is flawless. *Bluets* closed the 2000s, the chasm-2010s ushered by *Stag's Leap*. Catherine Broadwall's *Water Spell* mantles the Olds-Nelson altitude. Broadwall "[shows] up equally as a teacher, researcher, and artist" in this collection of lyric essays centered on media ekphrasis—*Amélie*, *WandaVision*, and *Final Fantasy X* among those flourishing in Catherine's dioramas on dragon-burnished stages. I want to buy a movie screen, furl it, bless it, then staple it to my campus library (the same school where Catherine received her Ph.D.), so readers may play the video games and watch the films referenced throughout this book that makes sea tomes of the cerulean-2020s. *Water Spell* is that nuanced.

—JON RICCIO
author of *Agoreography* and *The Orchid in Lieu of a Horse*

Water Spell is a hypnotic, kaleidoscopic meditation on rupture and repair, on the ways a life can shatter and the unexpected magic of putting it back together. Woven together in narrative strands, Catherine Broadwall's tapestry of loss and reinvention draws from the deep wells of mythology, fairy tale, and sci-fi's speculative horizons. With luminescent prose, Broadwall traces the fault lines of divorce and the alchemy of new love, carrying the reader across landscapes both internal and real—a new city, a new job, and a self reclaimed. *Water Spell* is a work of insight and beauty, a testament to the strange, incandescent patterns that emerge when we gather our broken pieces and begin again.

—MALIA COLLINS
University of Hawai'i Press

Catherine Broadwall's *Water Spell* interrogates the end of a marriage and the way one can silence their own heart. Ekphrasis is often a tool used when you can't look at something head on, you've got to come to it from a slant, while fragmentation does much the same, parts to a whole. Although both tools are deployed here, the effect is remarkably revealing. Broadwall writes, "I want to flush out the wound." And she does so, repeatedly, with vigor, until the water runs clear and you can see the exacting marks of where the blades cut and where you'll need to press your needle and thread to suture it together again.

—SHILO NIZIOLEK
author of *Fever* and *Little Deaths*

WATER SPELL

a memoir

Catherine Broadwall

CORNERSTONE PRESS
UNIVERSITY OF WISCONSIN-STEVENS POINT

Cornerstone Press, Stevens Point, Wisconsin 54481
Copyright © 2025 Catherine Broadwall
www.uwsp.edu/cornerstone

Printed in the United States of America by
Point Print and Design Studio, Stevens Point, Wisconsin

Library of Congress Control Number: 2025940334
ISBN: 978-1-960329-94-3

This is a work of nonfiction. All of the events in this book are true to the best of
the author's memories. Some names and identifying features have been changed to
protect the identity of certain parties. The author in no way represents any company,
corporation, or brand, mentioned herein. The views expressed in this book are solely
those of the author.

Cornerstone Press titles are produced in courses and internships offered by the
Department of English at the University of Wisconsin–Stevens Point.

DIRECTOR & PUBLISHER   EXECUTIVE EDITORS
Dr. Ross K. Tangedal   Jeff Snowbarger, Freesia McKee

EDITORIAL DIRECTOR   SENIOR EDITOR
Brett Hill   Ellie Atkinson

PRESS STAFF
Lillian Kulbeck, Sam Zajkowski, Kimberly Janesch, Karlie Harpold, Allison Lange,
Sophie McPherson, Ava Willett, Madison Schultz, Autumn Vine

*For anyone who has ever
received guidance or hope from stories.*

ALSO BY CATHERINE BROADWALL:

POETRY COLLECTIONS

Fulgurite
Shelter in Place

CHAPBOOKS & OTHER COLLECTIONS

Parallel
Feral Domesticity
Simple Magic
Coronations
Saint: A Post-Dystopian Hagiography
Gamer: A Role-Playing Poem
Flotsam

CONTENTS

Salt

The first thing I see upon returning to the house, having spent weeks away following my husband's walkout—complete with packed bag, like something from a sitcom—is the salt on the countertop. Big salt. Rock salt. The kind used to garnish glasses. Looking to the right, I see lime wedges in the compost bin. *Ah*, I think. *Margarita salt.* Unwiped. Uncleaned. Sitting there in clumps, like the remnants of something. Namely, our marriage.

* * *

THE WIND BLEW IT AWAY, our marriage. This is the line that echoes in my mind as I dash around the house trying light switches and finding no electricity. *Unbelievable*, I think. "It's too much," I say to God. "It's a heavy-handed metaphor. Fiction 101 stuff." Goosebumps prickle my arms as I search for the cat and try, for the third time, to call the husband—a man of mist, I see now, shrouded and elusive—who has walked out. I am met with crackling static. Even attempts at texts yield only "Message unsent" errors. I am alone in the frigid halls of the house while outside, leaves litter the yard. Tumbled-down branches decorate the streets. For blocks and blocks, there is no electricity. The wind blew it away.

"I get it," I say to God. "No light. No warmth. No communication. I get it. It's heavy-handed."

* * *

1

I WON'T REPEAT the things that were said about the kind of person I was, only that I find myself trembling in the shower, wishing I could cry, but somehow coming up empty. Like a well that is dry, I have no tears to give. But, upon stepping out of the tub, I see a red, slick cut just above my ankle bone. I nicked myself shaving. Blood trickles down.

Fascinated, as I have not seen my own blood in some time, I press my index finger to the wound. When I pull it back, I see the indents of my fingerprint perfectly outlined in red. I stare for a moment, then, moving on instinct, press it against the ceramic of the sink, right below where the spout starts.

"Remember me," I say. This is the only command I give. With this, I charge the blood spell. The most potent kind, I have read.

I do not charge it with anger. I do not charge it with rage. "Remember me," is all I say.

And yet, this feels like too much to ask.

Maybe this is how houses become haunted.

* * *

IN PACKING UP MY THINGS, I take very little. "I want to leave behind a museum of our marriage," I say to friends, through a smile a little too wide. Hilarious, right? A museum of our marriage. Behold, in Exhibit 1, the dishes my cousin gave us at our wedding, which we ate off nearly every day. Behold, in Exhibit 2, the couches we chose together. Remember all those video games and talks late into the night? Imagine the waxworks of us sitting there, simulating an era gone by.

As I fold a sweater to top off one of the cardboard boxes, a friend calls to check on me. She misremembers the phrase. "How's it going in the graveyard of your marriage?" she asks.

Something crumples in me like aluminum foil that is crushed in a fist, then discarded.

* * *

SALT CORRODES. It decays. It eats the bottoms out of cars, leaving latticed rust in its wake. In the Bible, Lot's wife turns to salt because she dares to look behind her at the home that is burning, a trophy of God's wrath. A testament to His immolating light.

Her husband went on, fleeing the scene, while she, the wife, turned to salt. Corroding the ground on which she stood.

I do not corrode. I keep my eyes forward. I photograph the beer can rings that are inches from coasters. "Like pawprints," I say to my brother.

I say, "I lost him to something. Some beast."

* * *

ON MY LAST NIGHT in the arid desert state where we lived, some friends throw me a goodbye party. We are eating in the yard when our phones buzz with warnings. A dust storm is coming. We are urged to go inside.

Though I have spent nearly a decade in the desert state, I have never seen a dust storm. *Fascinating*, I think. I photograph the leaf that hurtles onto my plate, narrowly missing pasta salad. I gaze at the quickly darkening skies. Once we move inside, I watch through the windows as the tree out front is buffeted, then pummeled, by earth and howling wind. Spirals of dirt beat this way and that. My friends pick twigs from their hair.

* * *

HAVING PUZZLE-PIECED together the sight of salt and lime wedges, I go on a scavenger hunt. I put on a smile a little too wide and crank up a frantic pop song. I know it must be here. Somewhere. The liquor. We didn't keep liquor in the house, but now that it is no longer *our* house, just *a* house, I know it must be here somewhere. They would not have been virgin margaritas.

I feel radiant, somehow, as I tear around the rooms. Joyous as I scour each shelf, each nook. I hunt in the shed. Behind the mixing bowls. There is no need to hide now. There is no need to hide anything. I whir in ecstatic conflagration.

* * *

AFTER THE DUST STORM, a friend drives me home. As we crest the hill that overlooks the city, lightning rips through the horizon. It looks like it is shooting up from the ground. Never have I seen such lightning.

"Heat lightning," my friend says. Never have I heard of it. It looks like the mountains are roaring their pain with teeth of shattering light.

We used to joke, he and I, that I was a weather witch. So this is my farewell—to him, to the state, to this life. So immaculately cindered.

* * *

IN THE END, I do not find the liquor. Maybe some things are too well-hidden. What I do find are beer bottles on top of the garbage, bottles in his office, beer caps on book-shelves. Coming back from the shed, I find that the rose bush he planted has produced one solitary bloom. A white rose, tiny and wet with spring dew. "Beauty and the Beast" is what comes to mind. Surely, this all must be punishment for something. For wanting. Like Beauty was punished for wanting a rose.

I wonder what it was that I wanted.

I do not look back at the city in flames. I keep running. I keep my eyes forward.

* * *

AFTER THE PARTY, after the heat lightning, I pack the final boxes alone. I do all right in the kitchen, the bedroom, the bathroom, the closets, the cupboards. But each time I go into his office, where I kept a few things, I immediately break down in tears. I fall to my knees. My hands press the carpet. As if something heavy is pushing down on me.

I call my mother and wail this into the phone. How every time I step across the threshold, it feels like something is glowering from the walls, laughing. Taunting. Jeering. Whatever I lost him to.

"Get a bowl of salt," she says. "Bring it in with you. Salt purifies things."

I fetch the bowl of salt and place it by my side while I shovel my journals into boxes. My figurines of heroes. I seal them with tape.

I see, in the corner, an object my father gave me: a Keyblade, a sword-sized key from a video game. In it, the hero fights creatures called The Heartless. I place this by my side too.

When I have finished packing, I gently lay the Keyblade across the office entrance. I want whatever is in there to know it may not follow me. I rub my eyes on my sleeve and brace myself to spend my last night in the house.

As I exit, I carry the bowl of salt to the bathroom. I turn on the faucet and wet my finger, then dip it into the salt. I scrub the ceramic where I had placed the blood spell, erasing its remnants. Replacing it.

"I wish you healing," I say. To him. To the beast. To the graveyard of our marriage.

We all have our own ways of fighting.

Trouble

I dreamt I was a tree, deep in a forest. My roots were wound around a boulder covered with moss and needles I had shed. A voice in the dream said, "See—you've become so accustomed to this pain, you've grown yourself around it."

Even then, my roots did not let the boulder go. Even then, they clung to it like a precious creature sheltered, a satchel held close to the chest.

* * *

I DO NOT KNOW how to speak about this. I do not know the word for watching someone I love become, voluntarily and involuntarily, swallowed by a garment they put on. I do not know the cry to make as the fur grows over their hands. I do not know what plea to scream as the collar grows over their face. As the line between the sleeve and their skin disappears.

A thing that transcends words. Words, the most reliable life raft I had known.

* * *

I DREAMT I WAS battling a beast in the woods. Snow made crystals on the ground. In the dream, I was flat on my back, lifting a shield with one exhausted arm. The beast pounded on it, scratched at it, knocking its jewels loose. It roared terribly, shaking snow from the bare branches. Its body moved,

reckless and relentless. But the eyes were those of someone
I loved. In anguish. As horrified as I was.

The eyes spoke in words I do not know. The beast's breaths,
rising through the cold air in puffs, were words I do not know.

* * *

I DO NOT KNOW what to say when someone I love says, voice
shaking, "If it is here, I will drink it"—then goes to the
market, returns home, and fills the shelves with it. When
my questioning of this, soft as a sparrow, is met with snarls
and barks.

Who am I speaking to, in these moments? The person,
or the beast?

* * *

HOW MANY MONSTERS can a heart contain? How many selves
can dwell there? I imagine myself the way the beast must
have seen me—a hindrance, a noisy gnat.

I imagine myself the way the person must have seen me,
but here, there is only a void. I imagine myself as two eyes
pleading, the silence of lifting a shield.

* * *

WHEN EVERYTHING EXPLODES, when the powder keg of the
home finally flashes into cinders, I dream I am hanging from
a single board of its wreckage, dangling over a cliff. Smoke
pours from the ruins of the home. The board I am gripping
is charcoal. A voice in the dream whispers to me, "All you
have to do is let go."

I know I will hit every rock on the way down. I know the
sea is there to catch me.

I unlock my fingers like roots from the board. I fall and
fall and fall.

* * *

FOAM AND SALT SLICE every red wound. I float on my back,
gaze skyward. I have no name for the pillar of smoke at the

cliff's edge that used to be a home. I have no name for the absence of a figure that might have stood there and gazed back.

I swim because the stars have no language, just presence. I swim because the waves have no words, just a pulse. I swim because my own heart is present and pulsing. I let these things carry me on.

Tropes

The day we separate our joint account into two bearing our own names, I thank God my brother was able to come to town to stay with me in the house. My first purchase with my new, single-person account consists of two vegetarian pizzas, ordered via a food delivery service. I cry while pushing the buttons.

When the pizzas arrive, they come in enormous boxes—comically large, as big as end tables. We are baffled by their scale. I check the order and see that there is no size option offered by the restaurant—just "pizza." Evidently, the pizza is gargantuan.

As we chew artichoke hearts and alfredo sauce and marvel at the boxes—so huge, they won't fit in the fridge—I am grateful that I am not in this moment alone. That as stomach-churning as it is to place an order from an account with the travel savings divided, the nest egg split, everything half of what it was just hours ago, I am not alone. I am here accompanied by someone I love. The universe saw fit to send uproariously large pizza.

I am not alone. Not alone. Love made a net, and I am caught.

* * *

AS WE FINISH EATING, my brother says, "You know, maybe this is like that trope in movies where one character is mean to another because they think it's for their own good. Like, they're mean on the outside even if they're sad on the inside, because they think it's the only way to get the other person away from them. Because staying would mean danger."

I know the trope he means, and I've always bristled at the way it risks excusing viciousness. But because the recent events in my own life have shaken me so much, part of me briefly entertains the thought.

Could this be what it was? Is this what he was doing? Fiction trope-ing me?

In honesty, I don't think so. And even if it were, it wouldn't excuse the mistreatment. But if on some small, subconscious level it were true, what danger would he have been insisting I escape?

Tethered

Ekphrasis on *Kingdom Hearts*

Once—only once—he speaks of it lucidly. It is winter, and we have just come home from singing karaoke. I am caught off guard because I thought we were having a good night. We sit on the couch with only the hall light on behind us, casting the room in an uncanny glow and obscuring his features, our faces being pointed toward darkness. He says it is worse than he wants to admit. Says he has rules for himself and that so long as he abides by those rules, he can tell himself it is not a problem. Says it changes its shape in order to stay alive—that when I attempt to impose a boundary on it, it finds ways to observe that boundary while squiggling out somewhere else. *It changes its shape to stay alive.* Says it has wound itself around him to the root, so that the place where it ends and he begins is indistinguishable.

This is when I come to know something of the shape of the beast.

What comes to mind as he speaks is a character named Ansem from the video game *Kingdom Hearts*. Ansem is a man, but what rises up behind him during battles is a creature born from his shadow. It floats above him, gold eyes gleaming. It has enormous claws and wears bandages across its mouth. It has a hole in its chest, which I recognize now as a cup that can never, ever be filled. It wants to devour. It wants to consume. It wants to fill the unfillable hole. The creature moves with Ansem, protecting him, attacking on his behalf. They are connected. Joint. Two sharing a body.

Any time I mention this conversation in the future, try to express concern about it, I am told it was hyperbole, that I am grossly overreacting.

In the game, the monster is not always visible. Sometimes it just looks like a man.

Red

Ekphrasis on *Game of Thrones*

In recounting the final conversation we had, the worst conversation, I tell people I told him, "You didn't just kill this marriage; you desecrated it." To say this would have been very direct. Very forward. But in tracing the lines of the memory later with invisible fingers, I remember that actually, it was something else. What I said—sobbing, bent over the kitchen sink, head hung low, hands gripping the edge of the white tile—was, "I keep thinking of the Red Wedding from *Game of Thrones*. How they didn't just murder Robb. How they desecrated his body."

I kept thinking of that. I keep thinking of that. The way, in the medieval drama's infamous scene, Robb Stark's mother Catelyn knows something is wrong. She looks around anxiously, though they are at a Frey family wedding, wrapped in an atmosphere of celebration. She knows. She knows something is wrong. When she lifts up the sleeve of the man sitting next to her and sees that he is wearing chain link armor, she is hardly surprised. It only confirms what she feared. What she sensed. That there was about to be a bloodbath. This doesn't reduce her horror. But she knew. She knew.

The Freys perceive themselves to be slighted, so they feel justified in murdering the Starks. But they do it so dishonorably that even in this land cut by swords and painted with blood, the surrounding kingdoms hold their noses in distaste. The Freys lure the Starks into a false sense of security. *Come,* they imply. *Drink with us. You are safe here. Dance in our halls.*

It is not enough to kill Robb. The Freys feel the need to humiliate him. Deconstruct him. Dance on his grave, so to speak. They feel justified in replacing his head with that of a wolf, the creature on his family banner, strapping his body to a horse and riding it through the grounds as the Frey army laughs and cheers. This is the image I could not stop thinking about. The way death wasn't enough. The way it had to come to desecration.

* * *

THE DAY BEFORE returning to the desert state for our last conversation, the necessary final trip, I vomited all day. At the time, I thought it was food poisoning. Now, I don't know what it was. Can a person make themselves that physically sick from anxiety alone? If so, my body must have known. It knew. It had seen the chain mail up his sleeve.

This moment is fixed like a fly in honey, as if held in suspended animation: with each declaration that comes, enumerating the ways I am unworthy, I envision a cut appearing on my psychic body. I do not reach for this image; I do not "imagine" it—rather, I see it in my mind's eye in real time, as if I am watching it happen on a screen. Later, I will use the word "blistering" to describe the pain. Later, I will use the word "obliterating." Later, I will say it is the new ten on the pain scale. It felt like my bones would dissolve.

I know. I did not die. I know: this is all metaphoric. But this is what came to mind as I stood there over the sink.

I know. You cannot "kill" a marriage. A marriage does not have a body. But if, for a moment, I can speak of the invisible as if I could know it with the senses, I would say something that had been alive met a grisly end.

Ring Burial

The day I go to bury my wedding ring on the island where the man of mist and I met, it rains. Walking down the enormous hill that leads to the ferry terminal, I see the water churn, the gray sky hunched in clumps on the horizon. The blue archipelago floats like a pod of dreaming manatees in the distance. I go alone. Decisively. Swift as an arrow. The rain propels my shoulders with its fingers.

Waiting in line before boarding the boat, I put in headphones and listen to a playlist I made him years ago. After all, this is a funeral. I want to remember. I want to flush out the wound.

I am surprised at the anguish in the subtext of the songs. I had assembled it achingly but lovingly following a fight. I had asked him to make me one, too. Threads seeking to stitch some tether ripped from cloth to scraps. Threads that may as well have been tossed in a gully, threads cast into a well. I listen to the songs he collected for me. Hear the sorrow echo as each falls.

As the ship pulls away from the dock, I stand at the prow and use my phone's camera as a mirror. I want to see how I look in this moment, and how I look is terrible. The cold wind has gnawed my cheeks deathly pale. The shadows carve rivers in my forehead. Behind me is the city I loved, then left, then scrambled to return to for a decade. When the opportunity finally came in the form of a dream job, he ended up breaking away like driftwood splintered by an ax on a beach. In the camera are me and the city I love, silver and glassy and bright.

Since this is a funeral, I beckon to whatever emotions want to come. I imagine myself sitting at a desk and penning invitations to them all. Licking the seals of a hundred envelopes, stuffing notes in bottles on the sea. Come, Sadness. Come, Anger. Come, too, Relief. Come, Peace. Come, Gratitude. Come, Stillness. Somewhere in the foyer of my heart, they enter. I drape their rain-steeped coats over my arm.

The day he first kissed the back of my hand, trespassing over the border of friendship, I took the ferry too. I was young and tipsy. I removed my sandals and gazed over the railing. The summer wind grew sharp as the vessel picked up speed. The flesh around my chipped red nail polished toes soon dimmed with frigidity and night.

I can picture this ghost girl, fleeting and laughing, hurtling, destructive as an anchor. I keep my wits about me now. My hands are in my pockets. My shoes remain on my feet.

The ferry bobs up to the island's pier and I disembark, jostled by strollers and bikes. Though I have not wandered these streets in years, I remember the way to the grave. Muscle memory pulls me forward. I do not dawdle, except momentarily to gaze in the window of a wooden structure that used to be a pizzeria. I worked there, barely out of my teens—turquoise-haired, calling out orders. Smelling of oregano, burnt cheese. Now, it is a gift shop. In the window display is a bell jar brimming with false butterflies. I cannot tell if it is hopeful or morose: this flock of pinned, transient transformers.

I make my way through emerald pines and maples brushed with crimson. The crowd thins out as I leave the small downtown, and soon I am alone in the slick streets. Twilight clings to the air. I walk past the building where he and I met. I do not pause to look in. I walk to a secluded, forested area just around the corner. We would come here back then, brush hands amid the green. Miniature woods to get lost in. Dizzying hedge maze of want. Even then, I felt deserted in his presence. An aura of foreshadowing, like smoke before a fire. Anticipatory pre-haunting.

I step off the dirt path that winds through the ivy. The plants' roots cover the soil. As is typical for me, I have brought something overly gentle for the task at hand: a spoon instead of a spade. I push the roots sideways, not wanting to do harm. I dig up bits of earth. I pull out the ring from the metal tin that has held it since I removed it for the last time, along with a silk flower hairpiece I wore on our wedding day. I clip the flower to the ring and lower both into the hole. I do not hesitate. I spoon dirt over them. I pat the wet earth down.

I stand, brush off my knees, and ask whatever emotions have come to say a few words. To offer their eulogies, their roses or screams. Sadness falls at the gravesite while others watch, hands folded. Though Sadness is shaking, other attendants help her to her feet, dry her eyes. Love holds her in an embrace.

On the walk back to the terminal, I listen to a new playlist. One I have made for my future. I welcome a soft smile onto my lips and marvel at the mist as it glints in my hair.

Before boarding the ferry back across the water, I visit the market we used to shop at and purchase a red and gold apple. The kind that was my favorite as I careened toward burning. Juicy and greedy and sweet. I lift it to the past in a sober, clear-eyed toast. When I am finished, I throw away the core. It is no pomegranate, I no Persephone, but I know better than to eat with the dead.

Haunted Mall
Ekphrasis on Photographs by Seph Lawless

The shock of one life ending, sliced as if by guillotine, slowly bruises over to a dull thrum. Nightmares dwindle. Clustered panic attacks gradually space themselves out.

Still, sometimes, wandering grocery aisles, I am caught in my tracks like a rabbit, frozen stiff. The sight of certain coffee creamer, certain veggie burgers, locks me in place to the ground.

I ask myself why. I do not want to flee the answers, even if they fly out of me like screeching bats. Even if they scream through the purpling night. I want to confront them. To seek the truth. I want to know the name of the feeling.

It isn't quite grief. It isn't even sorrow. Not anger, nor nostalgia, nor regret. In searching for the feeling's name, what come to me aren't words, but images. Pictorial analogies. They rise as though conjured by some subliminal algorithm: *If you're feeling that, these might help tell you why!*

First are the abandoned malls made famous by Seph Lawless. His photographs are haunting: in one, snow has poured through a broken skylight, and the stilled escalator is a lumpy slide of ice. Nearby pillars flake with rust. Flanking the escalator, storefronts yawn into caverns dark as new moons. In some, plants droop, yellowed and un-watered. In many, blue glass lies shattered on the floor, gleaming like bits of arctic ice. In one, a painted ringleader gestures to a painted tent that once sold funnel cakes and corndogs. Underneath the big top, the lights are off. The ringleader gestures, now, to nothing.

The second image that floats into consciousness is a former coastal military base, overgrown with grass and time. My grandparents took me there often as a child, where I roamed the echoing barracks. Though the fort never saw combat, locals whisper of ghosts, and the grounds evoke palpable eeriness. Beyond the cracked stone and encroaching moss, the sea stretches on the horizon. The compound teems with the aura of a graveyard. One that also serves as a playground.

These spots once held whole reams of human chaos—kids clamoring for one more corndog, soldiers sitting tensely in the pine air. Those stories have ended, but the ruins remain. And it is not the presence of the ruins that unsettles, but the absence. The incongruity.

The batteries, poised for attacks that never came. The ringleader, gesturing to nothing. Potential and history, orbiting around static images, their lips tightly sealed. For though the places might remember, they cannot speak. All they can do is convey, wordlessly, by existing. Convey and imply. They bring to mind marbles clogging the necks of half-spent hourglasses. Below, all the things that happened there. Above, all the things that didn't. All the things that might have, but didn't, and won't, and therefore, can never be known.

I rotate the shopping cart away from the creamer. I do not pick up the veggie burgers. I do not fall into the spectral hourglass. I refuse to prowl my own green grounds, a ghostly soldier with a bayonet.

Something happened, something is over, and physical objects remain. Ribbons of words spiral out in both directions—the fairytale wolf holds one end in her teeth. The words keep spiraling out. On the opposite end, the

long-winded *might have,* the words are scrambled, are gar-
bled. The past and deleted future both want to speak, but all
you see is coffee creamer.

It is strange to stumble upon these structures in the landscape of myself. And maybe there is no name for this feeling:
the feeling of witnessing a ruin. The feeling is *Haunted Mall.*
The feeling, *Mossy Barracks.* The feeling of gesturing, remem-
bering the funnel cakes that used to warm and sustain. The
feeling of thinking that you were prepared, but no, the battle
was elsewhere.

Orbits

I don't remember how the conversation started, but what I do remember, vividly, is this: me asking the man of mist, several years into marriage, in a tone of indignation, "Hasn't there been anyone you've ever been in love with whose eyes you could look into and feel completely open, like your soul was bared, like your guard was completely down?" I remember feeling insistent, wanting to know, irritated that he might not have. I didn't quite realize what I was asking. Or, maybe I did.

"Yes," he answered, without hesitation. "Has there been someone like that for you?"

"Yes," I responded, also immediately. And we were both startled into silence. The truth sat heavy in the air of the room. We were not talking about each other.

I know, for me, there is only one person I would ever say this about. For the man of mist, I don't know. That is not for me to say. But it was clear we were not talking about each other.

What do you do with this kind of knowledge? Why did we get married in the first place?

If we knew this—that our hearts were capable of more— why did we get married in the first place?

It makes me wonder about the different reasons people come together. The different shapes a marriage might take. I

think about wedding rings, how they might be like orbits—
some circular, some elliptical. How orbits can alter over time.
How sometimes, things can crash.

The Relic

What is the difference between a ruin and a relic? Some things you can let go of, let fade into the past. And some things, you simply can't. A relic gets cherished. Even enshrined. It takes on heightened significance.

For me, such a relic came in the form of a t-shirt. It was sepia-colored, appropriate for an object so steeped in memory. I had held onto this shirt since I was a teenager, carried it with me through many moves. I never really *wore* it, but it stayed in a drawer. I glanced at it now and then.

Once, in the desert state, I tried to donate it. This was after I had been married for several years. Achingly, wincingly, I set it on top of a stack of clothes in a brown paper bag I intended to give away. But as soon as the bag went out to the car, I snatched the shirt from the top and ran—*ran*—it back inside. Instinctively. Ferociously.

I admitted to this in therapy, how I'd held onto the shirt for so long because I was wearing it in a certain photo with a certain boy nicknamed Cerulean. In the photo, we are young and in love and beaming. I admitted that in addition to the shirt, I glanced at this photo now and then. I feared it was the happiest I would ever look. I feared it was the happiest I would ever be. I could not let go of this shirt.

"I know that's…bad," I told the therapist, feeling ashamed. I searched her face for judgment. But instead, she gave me a knowing look.

"Keep the shirt, Catherine," she said.

* * *

THIS TRUTH SAT IN ME like a slumbering seed. When everything exploded, it bloomed.

Branches

Ekphrasis on *Crash Landing on You*

I am surprised, as I clear my father's guest room of my belongings, to find tears welling in my eyes. In the wake of the explosion, I have been living out of a suitcase for the past three months, staying with friends and family up and down the east and west coasts while I wait to receive the keys to my new home. I have woken up not knowing what state I am in, fumbling for light switches on various walls. But my father's house is where I have spent the most time, the place where I have had my mail forwarded. My HQ, so to speak. In packing up the guest room, I feel my guts being wrenched. Like a pumpkin whose innards are scraped clean with a ridged spoon, leaving just startled, raw flesh.

I am saying goodbye to a home yet again. Some river comes undammed. Despite my best efforts, my eyes are wet as I roll my bag out the door.

In the driveway, none other than Cerulean is waiting. He sees my tear-drenched face. As I climb into the passenger seat of his car, his expression breaks into pity.

This is the person I have longed for, deeply, for decades, though I tamped the feeling down. The person I meant when I said that yes, there had been someone into whose eyes I could gaze and feel complete peace and trust. I tamped the feeling down until I did not have to. Until everything exploded.

He takes my hand and squeezes it. Then, "Look," he says quietly. "Look." His fingers move to his phone on the dashboard. He opens Google Maps and edits the marker for "Home" so that it is the address of the place we are moving into together. He sets it as the destination. This makes me cry even harder.

As we pull out of the cul-de-sac and move onto the highway, I apologize through sobs. I am holding his arm more tightly than I have ever held onto anything.

"I'm sorry," I say. "I'm so sorry. I didn't want it to be this way. I wanted to float down gently into your life. I didn't want it to be like the scenes in the movies where the spaceship is crashing into the ground and the windshield is covered in dirt and it's ripping up fields and everyone is screaming. I'm sorry."

He is silent for a moment, then says, "No. It's not like that." His eyes watch the highway. "It's more just like you floated down and got a little stuck in a tree."

This is a reference to *Crash Landing on You,* a romantic drama we have been watching. In it, successful fashion designer Yoon Se-ri, who lives in South Korea, gets swept up in a storm while paragliding and accidentally lands in North Korea, where the soldier Ri Jeong-hyeok finds her tangled in branches above a stream. As the series progresses, the two fall in love.

When Jeong-hyeok comes upon Se-ri, she is not at her best. She is windswept, distressed, ensnared in demolished outdoor gear. He has every reason to be wary of her. He *is* wary of her. And yet, he feels affection for her, even in her plight.

He helps her down. He treats her with kindness. He sees the good in her.

What Cerulean said was the perfect thing.

I don't know what I did to deserve this. To have my wet face and stampeding heart held so tenderly.

I sniff and murmur, "Thank you." The headlights cut through the clear summer night and guide us safely home.

Heart of Flame
Ekphrasis on *Howl's Moving Castle*

In the Studio Ghibli movie *Howl's Moving Castle*, a man's heart takes the shape of flame. As a boy, Howl swallows a celestial spirit who offers him magic in exchange for a physical body. The spirit uses Howl's heart as that body, flickering around the indiscernible lump that used to beat in the boy's chest. Its true identity is kept secret. What others see, for years and years, is a fire around a mysterious coal—a permanent, luminous flame.

A character known as the Witch of the Waste used to be Howl's lover. But even she does not know about the external heart. When the two cross paths years after their relationship ends, she simply gazes, enchanted, at the flame. She murmurs that it is a beautiful fire. Repeatedly. Her eyes shine bright, enraptured.

In the end, it is another woman, Sophie, who frees Howl's heart. At one point, the Witch realizes what the coal-heart is and grasps it to her breast, despite its plume of flame scalding her. She covets it that much. Does not want to give it up. Eventually, Sophie must coax it from her so she can return it to Howl's chest.

Watching this film in the desert state years before everything exploded, I was haunted by this image. A woman, rushed to old age by magic, longing visibly for a heart. I was less afraid of the scene where she snatches the flame—afraid, far more, of the one where she simply, visibly longs. Happily, confusedly, run through with pain.

Such a beautiful fire. The scene would echo in my mind as I lingered, mid-scroll, for just a moment, on a photo of Cerulean's on social media. Such a beautiful fire. Such a beautiful heart. I felt my eyes cease to blink.

I categorized this as a harmless crush on someone I had known since age fourteen. A boxed, tamed feeling that could not harm me, could not harm the marriage. A spark I had no intent to act on. I valued my oath and believed that effort and investment would save everything, would patch the ragged holes. Even as I felt waves creep in.

Still, it strained. It strained against my chest.

I was afraid, frequently, I would ask for him on my death-bed. And no one there would know his name.

Bluest Sky

Ekphrasis on *Demon Slayer:*
Kimetsu no Yaiba – The Movie: Mugen Train

In the 2020 *Demon Slayer* movie—the extension of an anime series—a monster manipulates four children into doing his bidding. They are orphaned children with fatal diseases. The monster's bargain is this: he cannot cure their illnesses, but he will send them into an eternal slumber where they will be free from suffering. They will have pleasant dreams, easy dreams. And all they have to do is infiltrate four demon slayers' subconsciouses and quietly end their lives.

This is how the demon convinces the children to slip into the heroes' dreams on a mission to destroy the floating, crystalline orbs containing their life force. The dreams, he explains, have borders that can be pierced, and beyond their boundaries lies the realm of the subconscious. That is where the floating orbs can be located and broken.

The children don't want to do this, but their own trauma is driving them. They are feeling hopeless. Their bodies are in pain.

As each child enters their assigned demon slayer's mindscape, we see the heroes' dreams and subconsciouses. Some of these are played for laughs; others are serious. One character dreams of romance in a sunny orchard, but his subconscious is total darkness. A figure wanders the void there, snipping a pair of scissors. Another dreams of his drunken father and cherished little brother. His crystal orb floats in a cobblestone courtyard brimming with barely contained flames.

These scenes invite a feeling of suspense about what the main hero, Tanjiro's, subconscious will be like. He dreams of his deceased family—family killed by demons. With so much loss in his past, and with such bizarre inner landscapes having been shown for his friends, anticipation builds about how his subliminal mind will appear.

When the child assigned to him finally pierces the border of Tanjiro's dream, what he finds on the other side is a pristine horizon, blue sky reflected in impeccable waters below. There is no land, only heaven and sea. The boy pauses in his mission, shocked and amazed by the sight.

When small beings made of light take the boy's hand and lead him to Tanjiro's crystal orb, trusting him even though he is an uninvited guest, the boy falls to his knees and weeps. He is overcome. He puts away his weapon. *Humility* is the word that comes to mind when I watch this scene. The boy is completely humbled.

Later in the movie, Tanjiro names the spell that defeats the demon after this boundless blue sky. Tranquility externalized, it burns with the force of a sun. Illuminates the way forward.

This is how I feel, gazing at Cerulean's heart. Reverent. Wonderstruck. Humbled.

One evening over a glass of wine, after unpacking some boxes, we are joking about a poor grade he received as a boy. I lean forward and blurt out spontaneously, "If I were to give you a report card, I would say your heart is a lighthouse." I am startled by the truth in the words.

Beholding this sky, my hands release all defenses. My knees hit the waters in awe.

Genre Studies

L eo Tolstoy famously writes that happy families are similar, while miserable families are unique in their misery.
But I wonder about this. I wonder what it does to the conversation surrounding happiness, unhappiness, and art.

Not including the extra classes I devoured in high school,
I spent twelve years studying literature and creative writing
in academic settings. I joke with friends that I am playing
Pokémon with English degrees, trying to catch them all. If
I were to include the years outside of classes spent teaching, reading, and writing, the number would be closer to
twenty. Over half my life. I finally embraced the English
major during my undergrad years because within my roiling
indecision about what path to pursue was a single, common
thread: courses about literature. About stories and ideas,
philosophies of life. Discussions of what made a piece of
art meaningful, beautiful, and enduring.

In these classes, it was almost a given that the things we
would read would be sad. "Sad" oversimplifies it, but that is
how it sometimes gets summed up. "Is everything we read
going to be this sad?" I have had students ask. "Everything
my teachers assigned in school was so depressing," people
have told me, as to why they didn't enjoy English classes.
The turbulent times we are in have made me take a step
back and consider what texts I assign. There is only so much

students can take. There is only so much *I* can take. The world feels fragile. During the early days of the pandemic, I helplessly watched people weep on video calls. This causes me to question not necessarily the usefulness, but the pervasiveness—the uniformity—of the many sad tricks in my bag.

I am grateful for my training—immensely so. Also, though, I wonder why my training has equipped me with so many studies of grief, disconnection, and defeat.

Are all happy families really so similar? Is that really all there is to say about them?

I can hear, as I write this, counterarguments in my head. I am a proponent of many of them myself. "Toxic positivity" is one immediate red flag. To study happiness at the expense of unhappiness is to shy away from discomfort, perhaps, but what is there to be learned from that discomfort? Many necessary, urgent, essential things. Systemic injustice and its historical roots. Personal pain that is microcosmic of larger, political pain. Toxic positivity attempts to ignore the countless wrongs the world is still facing. Racism. Sexism. Homophobia. Transphobia. Ableism. Classism. The climate crisis. Animal abuse. The concentration of power in the hands of a few. Many, many things.

But in addition to this, there is a bias, I think, against writing too rooted in happiness. In a widely-shared article from 2014, Ruth Graham admonishes adult readers of young adult literature (YA), claiming that its appeal runs counter to that of adult fiction. I think of this argument often. Graham seems to insist that YA centers happiness, though it doesn't, at least not always. In her book-length study of the genre, Roberta Seelinger Trites argues that actually, it centers power.

Adulthood does not guarantee happy endings, and confronting that fact can, indeed, bring a certain type of catharsis. Exploring the complexities of ambivalence, ambiguity, and uncertainty—studying these things closely, as if under a microscope—can bring a certain type of pleasure.

It is one I am intimately familiar with. One I am practiced in. I study sorrow under the microscope of myself all the time. And it has brought me a kind of pleasure, one that I once described to a friend as the pleasure that might come from seeing a demon exorcised. In the face of instability and inevitable loss—facts of life on varying scales for everyone, I'd say—examining pain carefully can help people come to terms with it.

However, I do think it's significant that a narrative that turns the corner into healing from that pain—examines what it looks like to heal from that pain—suddenly hops genres, according to common frameworks. It becomes a "feel-good" movie. Not "serious," not "literary." Soft. As if healing itself is soft. As if the only thing worth doing, the only thing possible, is unendingly probing the wound.

What I'm saying is that studying in the ways I have has not well-equipped me to be a person who experiences joy. And I wonder if that leaning is the chicken or the egg.

I think of the meme "Hide the Pain Harold," in which stock photo model András Arató smiles at the camera with a grin that looks more like a grimace, exhaustion seeming to lurk behind his eyes, and how the image reflects so aptly what is widely offered up as the true nature of happiness— the illusory nature of it, the desperation it belies. "This," many works I have studied seem to tell me, "is the real face of happiness. Transparently hiding anguish. A mask."

Happiness, in these terms, is suspicious. Weak. Its wearer must be in denial. Upholding, enveloped in, and simultaneously betrayed by uncritical ideas about joy. The white picket fence, perhaps. The monotony it connotes. Its steel fist of conformity.

I, myself, have been wary of happiness. Watching *Teen Titans* growing up, I liked Raven more than Starfire. Watching *Frozen* as an adult, I relate more to Elsa than Anna. I am naturally more drawn to the quiet introverts who seem to brood and be cautious with their trust than the bubbly ones who always seem to have sunny answers.

But is this just another dichotomy? An attempt at cleaving people from themselves? Doesn't everyone get to be both sometimes? Does joy always have to be framed as simple, as easy?

I remember, on January 20, 2021, watching Amanda Gorman recite her poem "The Hill We Climb." Her yellow coat and red headband made me think of miraculous marigolds in winter. Her hands danced through the wind as her words described a country that was flawed, but not hopeless. Disturbing, but not doomed. To me, her performance changed something in the air. This was two weeks after the Capitol attack. Two weeks. On January 6, 2021, all I could do was let my jaw drop in horror. Having faith in the country two weeks after that, I thought—that is astonishing strength. Nothing simple or easy about it. It is stunning. A stunning feat of hope.

At the start of the pandemic, I had heard people discuss delight as a subversive, vital, and necessary force. Delight as a tool for survival, for change. Nothing simple or easy about it.

Writers have explored this topic too, how making space for softness, healing, and pleasure can ripple out and change cultures for the better. Ross Gay, Adrienne Maree Brown, Jenny Odell, and Claire Vaye Watkins have inspired me on this topic, just to name a few.

I don't believe happy families are uniform. I don't think happiness is that simple. Are there shallow, surface-level definitions of happiness out there? Certainly. Are some of those definitions bound up in marketing and profit and hegemony and ill intent? Of course. But all the more reason, then, to excavate happiness from beneath that syrupy coating. I want to know the face of joy beyond corporate slogans. I want to understand what joy feels like to me.

After all, it was for lack of understanding of my own happiness that I suffered the way I did.

I want to know if joy is as complex a phenomenon as sorrow. I want to study it, revel in it, bend my mind toward it. I want to see what makes joy tick. I want to know it as thoroughly as I have trained myself to know pain.

The Woods

Though the narrative in the desert state was that I was maudlin, sorrowful, a canopy of branches obscuring everyone's sunshine, I think back on days I spent singing to the cat, baking pastries, rolling beeswax candles. Wandering back from walks along the river with library books in my hands. Picking paint colors to make the house in the desert state more beautiful, more ours. Spending hours scrolling through online catalogues of curtains, bedspreads, pillows. I think back on choosing cabinet knobs, each one different from the rest—a goal I'd had since girlhood—thinking, *Here is the place where I can finally do it, the place where I can make a house a home.*

I left everything. All of it. I took my books. I took only what I had come with.

When I came to the desert state, having moved across the country mid-Ph.D. program, I did not land in soft brush, but in quicksand. Despite months of long-distance going all right while I prepared for the move, once I arrived, I was met with put-downs, silence. I was taken to events where glass shattered at my feet, bottles thrown by whooping men on a porch in silhouette. Where the scent of urine rose from the lawn. Where beer cans littered the grass like dirty flowers, some tossed over fences into neighbors' yards.

The man of mist and I often walked home from these events, sometimes through inclement weather, because he was in no shape to drive and I had no license, driving being a phobia of mine since childhood. And I admit, this can be a frustrating trait. Or, at least, it helped weave the narrative I let myself absorb: I was childlike, burdensome, incompetent.

I admit it: in the desert state, I feared. I lived in an almost constant state of fear. When I attended protest after protest—small groups of us gathered on the capitol steps saying no, police brutality is not acceptable; no, no one should die in a mass shooting; no, the Earth is not a candy for you to lick away; so many other things—and counter-protestors brandished their assault rifles, glaring acidly back, I feared. I heeded the advice of more experienced activists: *Always wear shoes you can run in.*

As the climate around the 2020 presidential election grew more volatile, I feared. I wept into my hands one night, wondering aloud if I should get a tubal ligation in case war were to break out and I could not access birth control. (I asked once about the process at a doctor's appointment and had the question waved away, an irritating fly.) Watching me, the man of mist muttered that he did not know what to say. And I get it: to him, this must have sounded hyperbolic. It must have sounded like a breakdown.

Of course, this was before Roe was overturned.

After the divorce, I am diagnosed with generalized anxiety disorder and panic disorder, conditions I am told I have likely had for life. Not having that context, watching me hyperventilate as the school where I taught modified its student handbook to allow concealed weapons, watching me hyperventilate as yet another round of wolf-killing was rolled out, watching me hyperventilate as lawmakers told women to get back in the home—it must have been exhausting. It must have worn on him.

Believe me, it wore on me too.

I want to carry what is mine. I want to own my damage. I am by no means a perfect person. I have, at times, let trauma steer my hand. But I think about the nights I spent pleading for connection and getting glassy gazes in return, his lips to the bottle. I think about staring at the ceiling many nights, worried and sleepless and alone. Waiting for answers to texts that never came. I think about silver flasks poured into morning coffee, beer cans left in morning showers.

The narrative was that I was thorned branches, shadowed paths. But who got lost in whose woods?

Parallels
Ekphrasis on "Crystallized" Series and Instagram Photo

In the second spring of the pandemic, trying to keep our spirits up, I order the man of mist and myself a kit from artist Tyler Thrasher, whose "Crystallized" series has fascinated me for months. In Thrasher's photographs, crystals catalyzed through chemical reactions gleam through cracks in the carapaces of various beetles, glimmer on the wings of large and small moths, sparkle along the bones of a snake skeleton.

They feel reverent to me, honoring the lives that once were. In a class I taught on fairy tales, I showed the pictures to my students during the day we spent discussing themes of transformation.

The DIY kit offers the chance to grow crystals on a frond of eucalyptus. So it is that on a sunny day just weeks before my life is upended like a wine bottle hurtled to concrete, I follow the directions provided in the kit and watch crystals slowly form.

I am trying with all my might to grow something beautiful. I am trying to transform something.

In my fallibility, my excitement-turned-impatience, I mess up one step, failing to wait for water to boil. The resulting crystals are small. In the photo I take, they glitter on the branch I hold, running parallel to its shadow.

When Loving is Drowning

At first, after everything explodes, no words come. Only images. I make a photo diary of what is happening as a way to document it, remember it. Words are how I make sense of the world, but in the face of this eruption, words fail. There is only the image-maker, the camera, snapping rectangles of reality. A silent, mechanical recorder.

The first photograph on my phone—we had gotten new ones just a few weeks earlier—is of a hot pink rose jutting impudently through the extremely narrow slats of a wood fence. It is a single rose. Its stem is a vibrant, neon green. When I took it, I remember—heart feeling gouged open—hoping I could be that rose. Blooming defiantly.

There are other pictures too. The bent, distorted cover of a poetry magazine. I had handled it carefully, reading it gradually over weeks, but when I return after the power outage, I find it crumpled and mangled, as if it had fallen and lain like that for days. Somehow, this strikes me as telling.

There is a quail that appeared on top of the shed. I had never seen a quail in the desert state before. In the photograph, she rests in perfect stillness, ¾ angled, as if posing for a portrait. When I look up the symbolism of quails in dream encyclopedias, I am told they can represent everything from reunion to courage. Lust to luck. I still don't know what the quail means. But I chose to read it as a good sign.

* * *

THE OTHER THING I feel capable of doing before words come is make playlists. The playlist that helps me survive the summer is relentlessly upbeat, optimism distilled. Once the autumn comes, though—once things are calmer and I feel readier to gaze at the wound that has been ripped in me—I make a playlist called *what it was like (seeing the water)*.

In many of the classes I have taken, culture is compared to water, and we, the students, to fish. It is difficult for fish to perceive water because they are in water; it surrounds them. It is more or less invisible. It simply "is." The idea here is that although it may be difficult, we can learn to see the water. We can question whether what fills our lungs is healthy or unhealthy. I am trying to see the water. I am trying to understand. *what it was like* refers to struggling to love, painfully, a man of mist tethered to a beast. I want to know what it was like, removed from my assumption that it simply "was"—free-floating, adjective-less.

As I compile songs, threads emerge, unconsciously. Water, in fact. Drowning. Fire. Suffocation. Fragmentation. (When I do finally write, it only comes in these fragments.) There are motifs of oceans, caverns, and monsters. The image in my mind as I listen to the songs is of a woman having her head shoved underwater by a tentacled creature of shadow and salt. But, amid this, there are hopeful images too. Ones of life on land. Plum blossoms. Skyscrapers. Women setting down shards of glass and rinsing their own blood from their palms.

In "Good Morning," a song I had listened to often in the desert state without ever knowing the lyrics, Norah Jones sings of quitting a card game she is losing. Her voice is slow and peaceful, notes soaring out like a sunrise. I did not know it was a song about leaving a damaging relationship until I listened to it while sipping cold coffee on the floor of my new home, no furniture in sight. The mug reminding me of Baba Yaga's magic pestle that carries her far and wide—a fairy tale vessel sailing over treetops, containing her volume, her weight. The kind of thing that carries a person as they sit alone in an echoing room.

I set down my cards in the swirling whirlpool, the basement of the underwater palace. I set down my cards. I pick up my coat. I leave the light on and go.

Two-Toned
Ekphrasis on *Inside Out*

I think about John Keats' term *Negative Capability*, the way it honors uncertainty and mystery. The way it makes room for ambivalence, acknowledges the heart's twists and turns.

Like the multicolored ball at the end of Pixar's *Inside Out*, made from happy, gold feelings and sad, blue-tinged ones, emotions can sit in apparent contradiction but still make a certain sense. It's a sense that has nothing to do with logic. It moves to the rhythm of some other star.

I was not looking for my marriage to end. I was also relieved when it did.

Tilted

Ekphrasis on Wedding Photo

When I learn about The Big Lie, the one that changes everything, I almost hear a record warp. Reality slurs. My hands shake like static. A chapter abruptly ends.

* * *

DIVIDING MY THINGS into "donate" and "keep" piles, I see that a frame containing black and white photos from our wedding—an arrangement I made as a gift once—has been placed facedown while I was away. We pass like ships, occupy the house at different times as I try to straddle life in two states. I skitter like a stray cat, wake up in different time zones, toss and turn restlessly on different friends' couches. I fly back to the desert to sign papers, pack boxes. I hold in my hands one life ending, one beginning.

In one of the photos, I lean toward him while his body arches away. Surely, I should have read this as a sign. And it's not that it didn't concern me, sometimes. It's not that I didn't notice.

The blades we willingly shove from our minds, looking askance through saltwater and kelp. *A shell,* I must have convinced myself. Though the seaweed parted. *Just a shell.*

I resist the urge to pull the photos from the frame, write "SUCKER" on my face in every one with red marker.

I resist the urge. I put the frame down. I resist.

But only barely.

The Butterfly

Ekphrasis on *Demon Slayer: Kimetsu no Yaiba* the Series

Mostly, when everything explodes, there is just sadness. Of what anger does come, I cannot discern the shape.

I want to stop the cycle of suffering. To put it forgivingly to rest. But also, things have happened to me that I must work to understand. To not do so would let some grave go unmarked, forgotten in wind and time.

I try to discern the shape of my anger. I turn and turn it in light. Let colors refract off its million faces. Its prismatic, rainbowing points.

I study my anger by studying the character Shinobu from *Demon Slayer.* Her image occupies a precarious, uncertain place in my mind. If pop culture offers contemporary myths, an assortment of archetypal gods, I cannot tell what she is the deity of. The goddess of justice? The goddess of wrath? What is the shape of this anger?

In one early appearance, Shinobu floats down from the sky like an angel. She lands without a sound, dancing on ballerina toes beside a less-experienced demon slayer who has been fatally poisoned. Shinobu's black and purple hair is neatly styled. The pattern of her robe resembles butterfly wings. She wears an ever-present smile.

Shinobu administers the antidote quickly. She is composed, unpanicked. Though her arrival adds relief to the scene, there is something eerie in her calm. After all, this is an emergency.

Later, when she faces a humanoid spider demon, we see a new side of Shinobu. The way she blends ferocity and grace. Throughout the battle, her placid smile never leaves her face. Serenely, she asks the demon how many people she has killed. When the demon admits to five, Shinobu responds that she has seen the monster's wreckage on her journey. The number is actually eighty. Massacred. She smiles, tells the demon not to lie.

Shinobu says that the souls of those lost will not be able to rest until justice is served. She considers aloud how the demon might be punished. Some of the proposals are grisly. Torturous, in fact. At last, the demon has heard enough and lunges into an attack. The two clash, and the monster emerges, surprised to find herself with just a few cuts. But then she clutches her throat. Poison, Shinobu reveals, is her weapon of choice. Not brute force. Just a few drops on the blade.

*   *   *

WHEN I LEFT, I stripped the refrigerator door of all the things I had put there over the years. Postcards and magnets and flyers and notes. The only things that remained were two cards the man of mist had given me long ago, both bearing illustrations of anatomical hearts. Sepia and turquoise and red. I left them on the otherwise completely white door, precise as two needle marks.

Was this ugly? It was my most anger-filled act. Was it justice? What name do I give it?

*   *   *

ONLINE, I WATCH a video of Shinobu's battle. Words like *terrifying* recur in the comment section. But people also love her. *Favorite* shows up too.

I wonder if the contrast, the juxtaposition, is part of what leads to admirers' enjoyment. The butterfly woman vanquishing a demon, not a hair out of place.

To me, there is something satisfyingly gurlesque about it—*gurlesque* being a term coined by Lara Glenum and Arielle Greenberg to describe an aesthetic simultaneously hyperfeminine and grotesque. One that melds these things deliberately to disrupt common notions about what femininity can be. That reveals, perhaps, what it often is. Smiling and absolutely furious.

* * *

I WATCH A FAN VIDEO a user named Kittinette has made composed of clips of Shinobu set to the song "Angry Too" by Lola Blanc.

Blanc implies, in the song, that it is the discovery of concealed knowledge that has led to her anger. That anyone in her position would feel the same.

Shinobu composes her perfect, pink smile. Shinobu unsheathes her sword.

* * *

ONCE THE BATTLE IS OVER, in a moment of peace, Tanjiro and Shinobu sit on a rooftop gazing up at the stars. They are not good friends at this point. Just acquaintances. But after a pause in the conversation, Tanjiro asks, abruptly, if Shinobu is angry.

She is startled, and her smile fades for an instant. Then she answers that she is. She is, she confesses, immensely angry. Ever since her sister Kanae was killed during a battle. As a way to honor Kanae, who loved Shinobu's smile, she forces herself to seem calm.

I study this image. Smiling and furious. Graceful and enraged.

* * *

WHEN I LEARN ABOUT The Big Lie, the one that changes everything, the one that casts the entire history of the relationship in a different light and means I have been misled and deceived for years, a thousand impulses scorch through my mind of things that I might say. Ways I might react. Smiling, I contemplate these things as they bang around in the back of my thoughts—screaming, demanding to be heard. But also, there is a knot in my stomach at the thought of lashing out. Finally, a thought floats down like a feather: *Let's not have any more harming.*

Someone has to stop it. The cycle of hurting. I vowed, if ever given the chance, that I would be the one who did. The one who caught the rolling boulder of pain. The one who wouldn't strike back.

And yet, the heart cards were placed so precisely. Precise as two slim needles.

* * *

A WOMAN'S SMILE is no apolitical thing. Neither is a woman's anger. No woman I know hasn't been told at least once to sheathe her anger with a smile.

So it is powerful, I think, to see it unleashed—the anger coexisting with the smile. The rage-filled blend of restraint and release. Deference and defiance both.

I do not want to quell Shinobu's anger. I do not want to tell her she is overreacting. And yet, I agree with commenters that her treatment of the demon is unsettling. A little bit cat-and-mouse.

Where is the line between justice and vengeance? The heart cards stare from the door.

* * *

I CONTRAST SHINOBU's battle with one Tanjiro faces against another member of the same spider demon clan. In this case, as Tanjiro prepares to deliver the finishing blow, the demon, who has done harm to many, surrenders. She shuts her eyes, lowers her weapons. She doesn't want to be a demon anymore. He sees this. He changes the spell.

The demons, in this universe, were once human. Tanjiro consistently pities them. The enchantment he casts to
painlessly slay the demon is named for the sacred rain that
follows a drought. He ends the battle tranquilly. Even sadly.

Consistently, he finds his compassion. He wishes for their
souls to find peace.

Is this the difference? Does it come down to intent? Both
demon slayers resolve their conflicts, though their methods
diverge. But their adversaries had differences too. Tanjiro's
opponent had remorse; Shinobu's opponent had none.

I don't mean to always go looking for guidance from fictional battles. But what does sacred rain look like outside of
life-or-death combat? What is sacred rain in an emotional
struggle?

Where is the line between compassion and self-erasure?
What is the appropriate response?

* * *

THERE IS NOTHING apolitical about a woman's anger. Nothing apolitical about her smile. There is part of me that wants
to question the decision to frame a woman's fury as monstrous, a man's fury as just. A man's destruction as, somehow,
merciful.

Where is the woman who mercifully slays? Whose anger
gets to be righteous? What does it look like for a woman to
speak and not have it be taken as a threat?

How do I address betrayal without blowing a hole in
my soul?

* * *

I WANT TO SPEAK without a smile and not be met with
judgment. I want to speak without a smile and not be venom
or blade. The truth, I think, is the start of the spell against
internal demons who say, "You cannot." The truth rinses
the crusted blood. The truth is the first drop of sacred rain.

The Church of Alcohol

I dreamt I was deep in a humid swamp. Weeping willows brushed opaque ponds.

I picked my way to the vine-tangled entrance of a half-crumbled building, a hulk of gray stone. I pressed the door open, hands in lace gloves. A woman wearing a skeleton mask offered me a flickering torch. "It's a scavenger hunt," she said, a finger to her lips. But she did not give me a list of what it was I was meant to be searching for.

I took the torch in one hand, the mud-caked skirt of my gauzy gown in the other. I clacked through the hallways in satin heels. At last, I came to a room.

Inside was a church, hot and smelling of pinewood. People were packed in, swaying and singing. On the far side of the chamber was an altar. A preacher there lifted a beer on high, like a sacred Communion wafer. The bottle caught the hazy light that filtered through stained glass windows. A few of the panes were chipped or broken. Part of the roof was gone.

The congregants sang louder as an organ joined the tune. They raised their drinks—green cans, wine bottles, half-full liquor jugs—and jostled each other, some nearly falling over, in a slow and feverish hymn.

The heat was getting claustrophobic. Sweating flesh brushed my arms. I set my torch in a sconce and scanned the walls, trying to find a way out. The portal behind me seemed to have vanished. There was nothing but sanded pine.

The dream went on like this, my hands to the walls, the church's breath on my skin. I frantically searched, suppressing a scream, engulfed in singing, in praise.

Skin and Stone
Ekphrasis on *Song of the Sea*

In my new life, I watch the Irish film *Song of the Sea,* expecting to learn something from its depiction of selkies: shapeshifting seal-women. In various versions of the ancient myths that helped inspire the film, a selkie comes onto land in woman form, only to have her seal-skin coat that allows her to return to the sea snatched away in secret by a human man, who hides it. The man later coaxes the stranded selkie into marriage. In some versions of the story, they stay together for years. In some versions, there are even children. But always, the seal woman eventually finds her hidden coat and realizes she has been lied to. She returns to the ocean—enraged, I imagine—and lives out her days there. This seemed a fitting myth.

I don't need to say what The Big Lie was. But imagine it was something like this: something like the selkie finding her coat. Something that had been concealed for years, the discovery of which toppled trust. Something that meant that you had been lied to, long-term.

Imagine finding that coat.

* * *

WHAT INTERESTS ME most about this film, though, isn't actually its treatment of selkies. What interests me is the depiction of a man named Conor, who, in this case, has *not* stolen the seal-woman's skin. She has come to him voluntarily, and lives as a human until, one night, she has to go home. Something beyond her control compels her.

After losing his wife, Conor turns to drinking, the movie subtly implies. In the mythic allusions braided through the narrative, Conor is compared to a giant, Mac Lir, who allows himself to be turned to stone to mitigate his overflowing grief. He anesthetizes what he cannot bear to feel.

I know this. I know. Through research and reflection and support groups and conversation, I come to understand that substance misuse can be just as tragic for the user as it is for those around them. I understand that he had his own burdens, his own anguish. I understand that the movie's use of petrification as a metaphor for alcohol is apt because both can numb the heart, at least for a while.

I understand. I have sympathy. Still, it was painful. To be skin scraped against stone.

What Grows

O nce, when I visited him in the desert state long before I moved there, I scrubbed mold off his apartment wall. It was right above where he laid his head to rest. A blot of mold, sprawling and thick. While he was at work, I knelt and scrubbed the wall. When I told him this, he said nothing.

Later, after everything explodes, I sit at the dining table of our house, shellshocked. His night driving glasses sit folded there. I reach out and put them on. The lenses are filthy, smudged and blurred. With a pang, I think about cleaning them for him. But then I put them back.

Why was I always scrubbing away? What good did I think it would do? That relentless energy—where did it come from? And what was he thinking as he watched?

The Glass Coffin
Ekphrasis on "Sleeping Beauty" Tarot Card

O n the last day of 2020, I draw a card from Yoshi
Yoshitani's Tarot of the Divine, a deck my mother got
me for Christmas. The illustrations are gorgeous, depicting figures from fairy tales and other mythic stories from
around the world. I draw only one card, and it is Sleeping
Beauty—number XII. The Hanged Man, as it is known in
the traditional Arcana. In Yoshitani's image, a girl with a
scarlet blouse and a flowing aquamarine skirt lies upside
down, bare feet crossed at the top of the card. Her eyes are
shut. On her lips is a soft smile. Her hands rest over her belly,
forming a triangular gap with her thumbs and forefingers
just above her navel. All around her are twisting rose vines,
thorned and covered with buds. The roses are not yet open,
their petals tightly pursed.

The description of the card in the deck's guidebook is all
about hibernation. Waiting. Suspended animation. When I
look at this image on New Year's Eve, I do not have a strong
sense of what it means. It has been nine months since the
start of the pandemic, so I read the card as an acknowledg-
ment of stillness—the stillness I have dwelt in all year. I
have barely left the house, aside from short walks around the
neighborhood. Have practically lived at my computer, the

portal to my family, friends, and students. Indeed, I think, it has been a year of hesitation. Alive, despite being stilled.

I think, though, too, about the girl's young face, the way her hair spills around her on the pillow where she lies. I think about a poem I had recently written about a version of myself I had buried. A younger self, who looked like that. One whom, in the poem, I dug up.

* * *

WHILE COMPLETING my MFA remotely—eventually graduating online, as the pandemic prevented us from gathering in person—I kept picturing a silky cocoon. Going into the program, I was self-assured, headstrong. Came in battle-ready. I had earned a Ph.D. Had been teaching five, six, even seven classes a semester. Surely, by now, I knew how to roll up my sleeves and get academic work done.

But the program emphasized openness, wandering. Putting the compass away. Closing one's eyes in the deep, dark woods and letting some other power lead.

"I feel," I said, every few weeks, "like I will come out of this program different than how I came in. I feel like the program is changing me. But I don't know what I'll be when I come out."

"I feel," I said, repeatedly, "like something big is on the other side."

I could not have possibly known what.

* * *

OR, IF I DID, it was not with my mind.

Maybe some other appendage knew. Some feelers with which I sensed the world. A butterfly tongue rolling out like a red carpet, tasting a shift in the air.

* * *

IN THE OLD POEM, I dug up my adolescent self, and we sat in the dirt, embracing.

* * *

WHEN I WAS YOUNG, I loved Cerulean very much. We felt like watercolors overlapping. His quiet blue energy drew me like a clear lake I wanted to swim in forever. We were a couple for years. We bonded closely. But over time, forces outside our control put strains on us. Family pressure. Religious pressure. Another boy who was stalking me at school. A boy who showed up in my yard, self-harmed repeatedly, trying to convince me to date him. At sixteen, the compounded stress of these things left me screaming one night—literally, screaming on the floor—my hair splayed all around me.

My mother looked at me and called her friend, a spiritual counselor. "I need help," she said. "My daughter is having a nervous breakdown."

I remember staring at the wall, strands of hair over my eyes forming a nest, a net. Screaming until my throat was raw.

I was not the same after that. Part of me did not survive, or at least it was driven deep underground. A glass coffin. A rose-covered slumber. I became yet another fairy tale woman ensconced in petrified sleep. I told myself, *You are too much. Too damaged. Too chaotic. You are a burden. He deserves so much better than you.*

Feeling guilty and ashamed and furious at myself and like I could not be what he needed, I ended things in a state of complete dissociation. I felt outside my body. I felt made of dry weeds. Like some vital bird in me had fled. I was insistent. I thought I was saving him. I broke my own heart in the process.

We remained friends, but in the years that followed, I lurched through a series of unhealthy relationships, seeking some form of annihilation. Punishing myself, subjecting myself to all sorts of mistreatment, participating in all kinds of dysfunction, not understanding why.

"What if," I said, as I sat in Cerulean's car—after everything exploded, after I reached out to him, and by some miracle, he was willing to listen to what I had to say—"all my relationships after you were laments?"

Acts of silent screaming, howling at the sky. It turns out you can do this for nearly twenty years. It turns out you can call this a life.

It turns out you can even call this a marriage.

* * *

DURING THERAPY A FEW WEEKS before drawing the Tarot card on New Year's Eve, I cried, recalling the night I spent screaming at sixteen. I had never talked about it before to anyone. Ever.

But the pandemic had thrown my mortality into stark relief. I wanted to unearth the difficult things. I wanted to understand.

"Something was taken from us," I sobbed. "Because I wasn't strong enough. I wasn't strong enough to protect us."

Somewhere, the sound of a bolt unlocking, a glass lid creaking ajar.

* * *

IT TURNS OUT, IF YOU are angry enough with yourself, you can transform into a dragon. The kind that breathes fire, burning everything in sight, that is actually a howl of pain.

It turns out this can be taken for love: finding someone else whose screams are fire, too.

It turns out this can even look like stability: two dragons curled around a castle, the true sovereigns in hibernation.

* * *

I WEPT AS MY therapist listened on Zoom. In my mind's eye, a beam went up around me. The kind of thing that declares to the universe: *What has seemed dead has now re-awoken.*

I did not imagine it. More like I witnessed it. I felt the power in my words.

"I wasn't strong enough to protect us. *But*—I forgive myself. I don't have to stay broken."

* * *

THIS HAPPENS MONTHS before everything explodes. But I begin imagining dialogues between my current and younger self. In them, we sit knee to knee and converse.

She is so much more forgiving than I ever would have expected. Her movements flow like water, pulled by the grace of simply not hating herself.

*   *   *

I TAKE A BIG CHANCE. I try to talk to the man of mist about my revelations. I make myself very vulnerable. I know I am taking a risk. I tell him about what happened when I was younger—about Cerulean, how I lost him, how I blamed myself ever since—and say, "I think after that, I told myself the story that in love, I had no choice but to break and be broken. I think what happened distorted me so much, I told myself that was the only way. That because I was a bad girl for letting something beautiful be destroyed, I could only be with a bad boy."

"But," I say, tears in my eyes, "I don't want to break or be broken anymore. I want to cherish and be cherished. I think that actually, I'm not a bad girl at all, and maybe you're not such a bad boy." He had disparaged himself in such ways in the past. This had certainly been in the subtext of the story we told ourselves: that we were two rebel types, tough-hearted. But now, that all seemed horribly wrong.

I say, "I think we've both had lots of walls up, but maybe we could work to take them down."

I am not sure whether or not the two of us could have actually done this. But my epiphany had shown me I was raging around out of sorrow. I was willing to try.

"I want," I conclude, "gentleness and tenderness. I think maybe you do too."

The man of mist listened but said nothing. Just sat, expressionless. Looking back, I wonder if this was the moment I became intolerable to him.

I don't know how much I believe in vibrations, in energetic shifts, but I pictured, in that moment, my aura turning rose-quartz pink. Maybe this was when our color palettes blurred apart. We grew in different ways.

* * *

ON NEW YEAR'S DAY, the night after pulling the Sleeping Beauty card, I open my phone, still in bed, and open Instagram. The image that comes up is of Times Square, hazy-edged, black and white. Though the photo is not of my hometown in the Pacific Northwest, the cityscape galvanizes an ache that goes straight to my marrow. Regularly, around this time of year, I long for home, but this time it is palpable, urgent. I rise from bed. I go to the computer. Though the floodgates of the annual academic job market are typically closed by January, I visit a site that sometimes posts off-season listings. I search for posts in my hometown. And up comes a job.

It is a perfect job. A dream job. A listing that makes my breath catch. It is a job, specifically, in a department, specifically, that I have talked about with friends.

It is the listing that will end up turning cracks into ravines. The man of mist will not want me to take it. Despite originally agreeing that I should send in an application, as I advance through the first interview, then the second, his anger and coldness will grow. Barely a week after the third interview, he will walk out. I will not yet have an offer.

The prospect is just that, at that point: a prospect. Still, he will say, it does not matter. I am too emotional, too ruminating, too this, too that, too much.

I ask what would happen were I to withdraw the application. I ask what would happen were I to promise to never again apply for a job out of state. I want to—I have to—see how deep the ravines go. And no. It would not make a difference, he says. He storms out, saying he will "be in touch." I stare. *Is that it? Are we done?*

My young self watches like a ghost or an angel behind me, levitating, as he walks out the door.

A friend comes over after I call her in shocked tears. We sit on the scarlet couch. She holds my hands and says, "It's a new moon tonight. A chance to make choices. What do you really want?"

My young self and I lock eyes, hold the gaze.

"I want—" I stammer. "I want—"

*   *   *

FLASHBACK. MY WEDDING NIGHT. The man of mist is drinking with his friends while I cry in bed alone. I wonder how I got here, heart racing like a siren. What self-imposed sentence makes me think this is compulsory, I will not identify for years.

I went looking for trouble and found trouble, I will later summarize.

*   *   *

TIME PASSES. I am a few years into marriage. I strive for optimism, feed on the breadcrumbs of improvement. On visits back home, I go out of my way to avoid seeing the person who stirs up yearning. I have made a vow. I will keep my vow. Not just to be faithful, but to keep seeing the good, to keep telling myself the hopeful story. I promised this, when I made that vow: to keep telling myself the hopeful story.

Back in the desert state, I flinch at the snap of a can.

When does the hopeful story tip into denial?

*   *   *

MORE TIME PASSES. It is Valentine's Day. My husband and I have no plans. Cerulean texts to wish me luck on an academic milestone I have coming up. We text a bit about newfound loves in the form of movies and music.

Sweet pain like lightning flashes in my chest. *Oh*, I acknowledge. *Yes. Still.*

* * *

MORE YEARS PASS. I am deep in a dream where Cerulean and I are kissing. The dream my brain conjures is incredibly vivid. When I wake up, the texture of his lips still feels imprinted.

I shake off the dream. I rise and drink coffee. *A dream is just that*, I think. *A dream.*

* * *

SHORTLY BEFORE the pandemic starts, I find myself pacing by a river. In my mind's eye, I am a mountain lion prowling her cage at a zoo. Cerulean is going through a difficult time, and while I have reached out to offer support, I wrestle with myself over where to draw the line, over how much is acceptable to say.

"Do you ever," I say to my friend on the phone, pacing, stirring up leaves, "want to tell someone how much they mean to you—how important they are to you, how much you care for them—but not want to make it weird?"

"Well," my friend says, reading between the lines, "*is* it weird?"

The words disintegrate on my tongue. I fall silent. I keep it all in.

* * *

THE NIGHT OF the new moon: "I want—" I say. My young self stares. "I want—"

We both know what I want.

* * *

EARLY IN THE PANDEMIC, I catch the man of mist in several small lies about alcohol. As we shelter at home during those first nerve-wracking weeks, I wonder with horror how often I have been lied to, and whether it is just the forced proximity that reveals the pattern now.

Among other things, he drinks with strangers, unmasked, despite my pleas to be safe. Despite my pleas to help keep me safe.

My husband does not love me, I think. Semi-often.

I shake my head. Shake off the dream.

* * *

WHEN I LEARN ABOUT The Big Lie, the one that changes everything, two days after the walkout, I will be the one who calls it The End. Even after that, as a last resort, I will offer counseling, trial separation. I will try to do the diligent thing, try to do right by the vow. Each offer will be met with a no.

"CPR," a friend says. "Seems to me it was dead when you moved there. Everything else was CPR."

It turns out even this can be mistaken for affection: hammering on a cold chest.

Was this a kind of love? Two dragons scorching the earth and everything around them? Guarding, concealing, their slumbering selves? Striving, in their way, for connection? I think it was. The heart is vast. Love can mean many things.

It is true that I grieved for what was lost. It was a life. It was a life I lived.

* * *

WHAT I SAY, the night of the new moon, is, "I want this job." Somewhere, petals open.

And, my young self says. My mouth stays shut. But hers, the soul's, is open.

And—

* * *

AFTER WE DETERMINE THAT YES, it is The End, I wake up staring at the ceiling. Something is blooming inside my chest. Roses are everywhere.

I pick up my phone. I message Cerulean. I ask, "Do you have time to talk?"

* * *

I CANNOT SHAKE IT OFF as a dream anymore. I at least have to tell him. I have to say the words.

It was real. It was real. The realest thing I have known. Nothing has been more real since.

* * *

WHEN EVERYTHING EXPLODED, I was shoved from the cocoon, which was really a coffin anyway. I shut my eyes, moved deeper into the forest, put the compass in my pocket. Brambles caught my sleeves as I strode through the thicket. I followed some glow beneath my lids.

When I opened my eyes, I found myself at the bedside of a waking, messy-haired girl. She stretched and slung her legs over the edge. I knelt and drew my blade.

"This is for you," I say, presenting it to her. "Nearly twenty years' worth of struggle and growth. Take this power you did not have before. Cut your path. Do what you will."

The girl takes up the silver blade. The sun paints its tip magenta. Together, we walk to the castle gates. The doors groan open, sloughing dust.

She cuts a path through rows of thorns. Daylight warms our faces. Around me, the scent of fresh roses is astounding. We hold hands. She smiles at me.

* * *

ALL THAT SUMMER, the cocoon in cinders, I felt my body move on instinct. I did not question it. I let it lead the way. I let some other power take over.

Now, I see it. Rather than just bolting away from pain, I ran toward what called me as well. I threw myself toward it, ran headlong. I was running. I was running toward joy.

The Mind's Eye

I say "imagined." I say "pictured" or "envisioned" or "came to mind," but none of these are quite right. "Spontaneously saw" is more like it.

Synesthesia—a phenomenon where people's senses cross wires and overlap—can take many forms. People see music or taste words. The condition ranges in its manifestation and intensity. For me, for example, the months of the year have always appeared as certain colors when I picture their names in my mind. I have to organize foods in my fridge by complementary tastes—if I see pickles and chocolate syrup together, the taste of them prickles my tongue. Some song lyrics conjure mental images so distracting, I cannot listen to them.

Many celebrity-artists have said they experience synesthesia, such as Pharrell Williams, Stevie Wonder, Billie Eilish, and Lorde. These artists describe experiencing crossover between music and things like sight or touch. Author Holly Smale writes that she sees emotions as colors. This is the most similar account I have found to how my own perception works. Oftentimes—not all the time, but oftentimes—my emotions come accompanied by images.

In an interview for the American Psychological Association, neuropsychologist Julia Simner states that there are two kinds of synesthetes: projectors and associators.

Associator synesthetes whose brains cross color with other senses experience those colors inside their mind's eye, while projector synesthetes perceive the colors externally. She tells the story of one projector who assumed the lights went down during orchestra performances so people could better see the music's colors.

I am an associator, not a projector. But images come spontaneously, powerfully enough that they feel inextricable from my way of experiencing the world. Sometimes the images are of my own creation. Sometimes my mind pulls from what it has seen, offering pictures or clips from media as if drawing from a huge rolodex.

Though synesthesia does seem to have a genetic component, a report by Carl Zimmer in *The New York Times* suggests that the mind's eye can be worked like a muscle as well. In my case, I suspect it is partly inherent, partly something I have built. The colors of the month correspond to a calendar I remember making painstakingly in school as a child. January is forever blue and white because I drew snowflakes around the word against a winter sky. February is pink and red because I drew Valentine's Day hearts. To this day, I cannot see October as anything but orange and black. It is pumpkins and witch hats. It's not that these are uncommon associations—I'm sure lots of kids drew the same things. But studies suggest that some people's brains lock the associations in place more tightly. I picture or hear the word "February," and my mind's eye pulls up red hearts.

Likewise, I remember my parents taking me to a show at a planetarium when I was very young—four or five—that paired the music of Sergei Prokofiev's *Peter and the Wolf* with abstract, squiggly art. Already, in the orchestral composition, each character corresponds to an instrument: the bird is a flute, the cat a clarinet, the grandfather a low bassoon. In the planetarium show, those associations were further expanded by adding in visual patterns. I think the duck was a golden ribbon, the hunters ripples of red.

So maybe I was primed for this way of knowing the world, pressing feelings and pictures together. Brain scans show that synesthesia is an observable phenomenon. But how the mind's eye works and its relation to brain development, including neurodivergence, is still not completely understood.

Zimmer also talks about a condition called hyperphantasia: an unusually strong mind's eye. He distinguishes it from vivid imaginings, explaining that people with hyperphantasia can experience memories, including scenes from movies, in almost photographic detail. There is also a condition called aphantasia, where people have little or no mind's eye at all.

I think I have a touch of hyperphantasia, a touch of synesthesia. For whatever reason, my mind associates images with feelings, often inseparably.

* * *

THIS IS WHY I HAVE BEEN so drawn to ekphrasis as I have tried to make sense of my year of chaos and renewal. Laurie G. Kirszner and Stephen R. Mandell explain that ekphrasis, a term dating back to ancient Greece, refers to writing inspired by visual art. Poet Alfred Corn adds that ekphrasis should be grounded in a specific *encounter* with the art. The job of the writer is not just to summarize. The writing should reveal the observer.

Hence, we have Rainier Maria Rilke close his famous ekphrastic poem on a half-crumbled sculpture of Apollo with the poignant realization that he has to change his life. We don't just see the statue. We see the author, too. He offers his aching heart.

* * *

ACCORDING TO ZIMMER, the mind's eye can work to heighten emotion. Experiences seem to lodge more viscerally in people who do not have aphantasia than those who do, at least according to factors like skin conductance. One theory is that the mind's eye enables people to relive experiences visually, making them harder to forget or shake off.

When told about a new kind of procedure that might strengthen the mind's eye involving magnetic pulses and cognitive exercises, one man with aphantasia said he would not undergo it. Zimmer states that the man has no interest in being swallowed up abruptly by uninvited images.

Uninvited images: that is sometimes how it feels. Like my brain is drawing metaphors, preexisting and original, for every feeling I have. Like I perceive the world, almost, in film.

*   *   *

SIMNER REPORTS that synesthesia is correlated with creativity, even with artistic careers.

Also, she adds, it is correlated with anxiety disorders.

To visualize involuntarily—I do not know any other way. I am grateful for my metaphor-drawing mind and its oceans of feelings that swell up. I am grateful to the heart, with all its silent knowledge, the way it swims toward images to speak.

*   *   *

BIBLIOTHERAPY IS THE ART of using stories to understand oneself and one's pain. Bill Ellis coins the term *fairy-telling* to describe the weaving of new fairy tales inspired by older ones. In trying to piece myself back together, I suppose I am doing both.

As to why so many of the images and stories that come to mind for me are fantastical, I suspect it is because I am delighted by stories of magic. I joke (half-joke) that I want to create a major in Magical Girl Studies. To reflect on these stories gives me pleasure in a culture that too often separates them from "fine art." Reading reflections like Roxane Gay's on *The Hunger Games*, Carmen Maria Machado's on *The Little Mermaid*, and Jack Halberstam's on *Monsters, Inc.* gave me faith that this was possible—to write about these characters from a place of seriousness and care.

As Jennifer K. Stuller writes, such stories, including super-hero stories, contain powerful archetypes and other aspects of myths. These are the kinds of tall tales that might be told around campfires, their shadows stretching long.

Generally, I view magic as a metaphor for power, and I want to know what mine looks like and how to use it well. I have less than no interest in literal violence. I read all these things symbolically.

* * *

WHY ANIMATION? Why cartoons? What comes to mind is an idea from Scott McCloud. He writes that part of cartoons' power lies in their blend of simplicity and exaggeration—cartoons as kinds of myths. The medium lends itself to exaggeration, to heightened intensity.

I think I perceive difficult moments in cartoon. No, even more than that, I think I *feel* in cartoon.

Though images are sometimes considered "simpler" than words, and while larger-than-life stories are sometimes considered "simpler" than more realistic ones, I think both have power.

Once, I realized I liked poems and animation for the same reason. Anything can happen. Reality is elastic. Both are enchanted domains.

* * *

IN THEIR FAMOUS BOOK *Metaphors We Live By*, George Lakoff and Mark Johnson observe that many metaphors take inspiration from the sensory world—the tactile, embodied world. This idea may be truer for some than others, but for me, it resonates: metaphor is woven into my bones. I want to know these embodied truths. I want to let my tissue speak.

I know not all the images I reflect on here come from perfect sources. Several—along with the companies, and in some cases, people that made them—could stand to be critiqued. But they are ones I have encountered as I have swum in this culture's waters, ones that have impressed upon me. They are ones that have helped me navigate a year where my life turned upside down.

I am humbly looking to these images for guidance. I approach them as a student—I want to know what they might teach. My mind's eye and heart churn together, offer pictures. I walk the beach and lift them to my ear.

Storms
Ekphrasis on *Encanto*

We used to joke that I was a weather witch.

One spring, I received an alarming email. As I cried on the futon in the small apartment we then shared, the sun became engulfed in clouds and snow began to fall—softly, then quickly, until it surged at a forty-five-degree angle. As I gradually calmed down, the impromptu blizzard stopped. It was an anomaly. There was no snow before or after that for weeks. We laughed about it at the time, how emotion was a primordial force.

Another time, a hornet soared into our living room, and I thrust my hand toward it, saying, "Go away! Go to the light." Immediately, the hornet sailed into the ceiling lamp and smothered itself on the bulb. Its silhouette sat there, silent. My eyes widened in horror.

His did, too. *A lightning witch.* "Don't send *me* to the light," he said.

I don't believe I caused these things in a literal, logical sense. But as a student of literature, I am always on the lookout for symbols. Brushes of themes in my lived-in story. Traces of omniscient narration.

* * *

IN DISNEY'S ANIMATED FILM *Encanto*, the members of the Madrigal family have special, supernatural gifts. One character, Pepa, is a weather witch. Her moods affect the climate. Sunshine bursts through the windows when she's happy; storm clouds gather when she's not.

In a moment of distress, she tugs on her braid, stroking its curves, urging herself to picture a cloudless sky. Trying to soothe herself.

I recognize this at once. Others see it too: I read the word *anxiety* repeatedly in comment threads. Pepa's elemental, mercurial power is suggestive of an anxious temperament. She has constantly been told she is too much, too emotional. I watch her struggle to rein herself in.

She struggles, and yet, part of what moves me about the film is to see how lovingly she is treated. Yes, she is regarded as frustrating in moments, where characters complain about her rainclouds. But overall, she is cherished.

It touches me to see someone stormy be accepted. Allowed emotional range. Just depicting this, I think, is a powerful act. Just depicting this offers something.

* * *

WHEN I GET TOO ANXIOUS, I seem to break technology. Wi-Fi goes down. Computers won't start. As if stress is leaking from my fingertips through the gaps in the keyboards, riding currents of air. Sizzling fragile circuits. Including, sometimes, my own.

I understand: he heard thunder when my eyes welled. Retreated into what he thought offered shelter. Retracting, withdrawing. Battening hatches. Preparing for emotional typhoons.

But wasn't I sunny sometimes too? Didn't my laughter light something?

* * *

A FEW WEEKS after our house is no longer our house—just his house, my name removed—he writes to tell me of a plumbing disaster in the yard. The pipes underground, it seems, have erupted. The yard is flooded, earth clods gushing.

As I read, my mind's eye conjures an image of a woman bursting into tears. If this were a fairy tale, my sobs would have cosmically prompted the pipes to burst in sympathy.

I hear through the grapevine at one point, too, that he has tripped on a root. Something about falling by a river. Because I am not sleeping and I look for symbols everywhere, I hope I did not somehow cause this.

* * *

AFTER THE MOVE BACK to my hometown, I am startled by how often I am happy. Despite the narrative of me as a "frigid blizzard," I find myself breathing more easily. Inconveniences derail me less. I watch myself. I watch myself closely.

The climate of my moods slowly grows warmer as the pace of my frenzied life slows. I find it surprisingly easy to relax. I lounge. I sip tea and read books. Rather than correctional, atoning behavior, this feels like a truer self that had been long suppressed. *Circumstantial* is a word that comes up in therapy. *Circumstantial* self as storm.

I still have bad weather days. Moves and new jobs do not cure anxiety disorders. But the circumstances' change was immense.

* * *

I REMEMBER THE LIGHTNING screaming down from the sky the night before I left the state for good. Blistering the dry hills with scorching prongs of lavender. Wind knocking powerlines down.

Maybe this was a coincidence. Maybe it was my goodbye. If this were a fairy tale, I could glare over my shoulder and vanish in a flash of light, a chariot of leaves. If this were a fairy tale, I could weep and dissolve into forces as primal as grief: flood the yard with silted water, drown in a lakebed of tears. Let the earth take back my body, scatter to minerals and salt.

Instead, I swim. Follow the sun on the horizon. Pull through spangled waves. And maybe the wind at my back is conjured, the heart its own stratosphere.

Water Ritual
Ekphrasis on *Sailor Moon*

I stand before the mirror in a hotel bathroom, clouds and fir trees out the window. It is dusk. The horizon is tangerine and mauve. I am seeing Cerulean tomorrow. It will be the first time we see each other in person since I reached out to tell him how I feel.

I have not been alone in weeks, I realize, having stayed with my mother while I waited to hear from the job. It is the first time I have been alone—completely alone, without even a pet—in months.

I stare at my body as I prepare to enter the shower. Slowly, my fingers unscrew the knob at the top of my belly button piercing. I tug the metal bar out of the hole in my skin, where it has lodged for years. I gaze at the new gap it leaves above my navel. I bring the two halves of the jewelry together and rinse the stud in the sink. I scrub it gently with my fingers. Soap runs down the artificial gems, cut to resemble something real, but unreal. Imitation gems.

Cerulean texts and asks what I am up to. "A water ritual," I say.

* * *

I AM TWENTY-ONE. I am lying on my back on a raised platform in a piercing shop. I am here to have a navel stud put in. I am here because the man of mist said he liked the look of them once. I want to shine, to be enchanting. I will not ask why this requires pain. I will not ask what makes me lie here in repose, gouging out part of my flesh in the poisoned hope of catching his eye.

The metal goes in and what comes out is a tiny roll of skin, no thicker than a millimeter. Still, it surprises me. I have only had my ears pierced. I have never seen what gets displaced.

He will approve. I will keep it in for fourteen years. Even when our paths run parallel.

*　*　*

I AM TWENTY-TWO. The man of mist has moved away, our initial flash-in-the-pan of a fling concluded with a douse of ice. I am seeing someone new, self-destructively. He tries to convince me that my worldview is all wrong. He tells me he hates nose rings.

Immediately, defiantly, I go and get my nose pierced. The side of my face hurts all day.

The side of my face will hurt sporadically, a dull thrum. I will keep the piercing in for thirteen years.

*　*　*

I AM THIRTY-FIVE. I pull the nose stud out. I rinse it in the hotel's shining basin. I set the two piercings on a thin bed of tissue, then fold the paper up, throw them away. I do not do this angrily. I do not do it tearfully. I set them down in the empty bin and wash my unshaking hands.

The holes in my face and belly feel odd. But free, like a bit removed from a mouth. Airy like windows that had crusted shut being scrubbed and opened wide.

I asked at the hotel front desk for a razor. Now, I hold it in my hand. It is cornflower blue. I step into the shower. The razor has just one blade.

I don't know why I asked for a razor. I did it automatically, without asking why. Instinct moved, and I conceded.

I run the razor over my legs, the tiny blue stick a kind of reaper. Hot water pours down my back; steam rises. I take my time, let warmth fill my cheeks. I wash my hair with unfamiliar shampoo. I close my eyes and breathe.

There is no ritual I know for what I am doing, so I must design a new ritual. There is no rite of passage for shedding this skin, so I must use what resources I have. I think of what archetypes might relate to cleansing with water, what heroes might come to my aid.

What come to mind are two warriors from the earliest magical girl story I encountered: Sailor Mercury and Sailor Neptune from *Sailor Moon*. Both girls have blue hair and blue outfits. Both cast water spells. Mercury conjures torrents of ice; Neptune shoots oceanic spheres. Both are graceful and fierce.

Both would know what to do in this moment. I imagine their clarity, their strength. I call down the water to cascade on me. I watch the past spin down the drain.

Labyrinths
Ekphrasis on *WandaVision* and *Amélie*

I t starts with a house.
    At the beginning of Marvel's series *WandaVision*, we see Wanda Maximoff and her husband, Vision, driving to their new-bought home. They are also newly married. Wanda is still in her wedding gown, Vision still in his suit. Cans clatter on strings behind their car. The scene is filmed in black and white. The whole episode is black and white. In the style of a 1950s sitcom, Wanda must navigate preparing a perfect meal for Vision's boss and his wife. Wanda is a sorceress, Vision an android, so hijinks ensue. The episode ends with the pair smiling together on the sofa in their spotless living room.

Of course, fans of the Marvel Cinematic Universe know this is not right. Vision was murdered in a previous film. It is certainly not 1950. But what is amiss is concealed.

As the series progresses, so do the decades: the second episode is shot in the style of a 1960s sitcom, the third 1970s, and so on. As time advances, the narrative begins to glitch—a red toy helicopter intrudes on a black and white scene, a voice on the radio calls Wanda's name. She tilts her head, perplexed. One night, she and Vision hear a sound outside. They walk beyond their fence to the street. Out of a manhole crawls a person in a beekeeper's suit. Bees swarm around him. Wanda gazes at the figure, initially confused. Then her eyes grow icy. She sets her jaw. Says no. Responding to her disapproval, the scene freezes and reverses, distortions marring the screen, with the sound of a VHS tape rewinding.

Wanda wants so badly to control the narrative. She wants to make things right. She banishes the beekeeper, who is actually a secret agent, trying to remove her from the charming lie she has built.

* * *

IMAGINE ME PICKING OUT Art Nouveau prints, scrolling through paint colors to find the perfect blue. Imagine me framing photos from our wedding, placing them in prominent places, as if they could ward off indifference. As if I could cast a circle of protection. *If I just get the look of this right—*

* * *

IN THE EPISODE set in the 1980s, Vision starts asking questions, sensing that something is off. He has no memory of life before his marriage. He presses Wanda; she evades. She tries to leave the room. Credits start to roll over synthesizer music. She says she is going to bed.

Vision insists the discussion is not over. The credits and music stop. The couple quarrels, tensions rising until they use their superpowers to lift themselves off the ground. They hover in the air of their living room, eyes locked. Angry and confused, both feeling betrayed.

Wanda insists, voice taut with emotion, that everything she is doing is for them. All her desperation, all her effort. All her pain. All for them.

* * *

THE THERAPIST TELLS ME that part of grieving a relationship is grieving the dream you had for your shared life. The couple you thought you would be.

I remember watching the French movie *Amélie* with a kind of desperate hope. A "Hide the Pain Harold" hope, grinning through a sense of dread. This was right before everything exploded. I was seeking out art prints of the film's quirky couple, Amélie and Nino. Their aesthetic of photobooths and bicycle rides. Bright walls and curtains of beads. Fresh-baked plum cake in afternoon rainstorms. Hushed glances of understanding.

It was not meant to be. It was not a shared dream. I left behind the paint cans, the bag of baking flour. What became of them, I don't know.

I could never locate us in fictional couples. Could never find us up there on the screen. Maybe I should have seen this as a warning sign. The search was a river that mixed longing and sorrow in my chest, cold as wet rain down a neck. Amélie and Nino were always out of reach. Something I knew I could not grasp.

There was a song from *Amélie* on the playlist I made him, the one I listened to the day I went and buried my ring. I had forgotten all about it. It was several years old.

I suppose I had been dreaming a long time.

* * *

EVENTUALLY, IT IS REVEALED that Wanda has inadvertently engulfed a town called Westview in an enchanted space called a Hex. As a child growing up in war-torn eastern Europe, she was mesmerized by old American sitcoms. She viewed them as a source of comfort. Since then, she has lost her parents, her brother, and, finally, Vision to violence. So much loss. So much anguish.

Late in the series, we see the moment that led to the creation of the Hex. Wanda drives to a plot of land in Westview that Vision purchased before his death, where he meant to build them a home. Walking out into the patch of dirt, Wanda gazes at the blueprint of what might have been their house, alongside a hand-drawn heart. Grief overwhelms her. She falls to her knees and lets out a scream. From her hands and her heart and her mouth bursts red light, transforming the setting around her. Color turns to black and white. Cars revert seventy years. The plot of land, pixel by pixel, evolves into a beautiful home. Her husband emerges before her, smiling. The threads of reassurance from her childhood spool forward, sewing an engrossing tapestry. She yields to the fantasy of it.

When, eventually, Wanda gains some cognizance of what her magic is doing, she presses on anyway. Agents confront her, telling her she is holding the residents of Westview hostage in her fantasy as captive, living puppets. She refuses to hear it, to acknowledge the cracks in her utopia. The cost of it. The human toll.

* * *

IN THEIR ARTICLE "Becoming the Labyrinth: Negotiating Magical Space and Identity in *Puella Magi Madoka Magica*," Sara Cleto and Erin Kathleen Bahl focus on enchanted spaces called labyrinths that appear in the anime series mentioned in the title. Labyrinths are similar to Wanda's Hex. The biggest difference is that labyrinths are mobile, appearing when beings called witches are nearby. Protagonists can tell a witch is approaching when reality begins to warp. Nonsensical images appear out of nowhere: butterflies with rose bush wings, cotton balls with teeth. As the witch draws nearer, the images proliferate until they take up the entire screen. The labyrinths seem illogical, chaotic. But Cleto and Bahl argue that they are far from random collages. As the show goes on, witches are revealed to be the souls of grieving human girls who have woven mazes of protection around themselves. The labyrinths consist of images sourced from whatever trauma they have endured.

Cleto and Bahl write that in labyrinths, "remembrance and creative storytelling intersect to frame a space in which [a witch] can grieve and reestablish narrative control over her story."

This perfectly describes what Wanda is doing.

It describes what I am doing, too.

* * *

REPEATEDLY, Wanda pleads with Vision to embrace her narrative. That everything is perfect, is fine. That they are a happy couple in a happy home. She tries so hard to mend the rips. Her stubbornness a fire, a force. Wanda does not want to give up.

When people ask why I stayed so long, given all the fractures, I answer reflexively, "I made a vow." I did not want to give up.

I cried on the last day, the end of it all, "That anger and anxiety you saw over the years—it was grief. It was grief masquerading."

I picture Wanda, seething, pleading, pouring effort in. Roaring her pain, her corrupted, futile wish. Not asking what parts of herself she has silenced, taken hostage with the town.

Grief is what sustains the illusion. Grief is what stitches the Hex.

* * *

IF I JUST GET THE LOOK OF THIS RIGHT—me at a screen, eyes reflecting throw pillows. Looking up recipes for lady fingers, macarons. Collaging. Arranging. Grasping at straws. Spinning a maze of denial.

Once, I spent hours trying to get a cupboard to shut. The hinge was askew and the door wouldn't close the way I wanted—*needed*—it to. I exhausted screwdrivers, magnets, mounting putty, Velcro.

Perhaps I should have seen this, too, as a sign. It all felt very high-stakes.

* * *

WHAT FALLS IN THE GAP between a dream and reality? What rushes to fill in that chasm?

* * *

IN A 2014 ESSAY, Amber Sparks coins the term *domestic fabulism*. It refers to literature that borrows elements from fantastical genres but situates them within the setting of the home. It can reveal, Sparks explains, the precarious balance between domestic belonging and alienation.

Belonging, alienation. Wanda's gritted teeth. Her fury. Her tenderness. *I made a vow.*

It is this quality, I think, that makes the show feel so intimate. The stakes involve a home: a home collapsing. Wanda's impulse is sympathetic, her execution horribly misguided. Her magic spent simulating what can never be. Trying to claim control of her story. Trying to wrestle her grief.

This is a story of domestic fabulism: the home a site of longing, of power. Power that spins wild narratives like red shrouds, that raises living memories with will.

Perhaps the same could be said of any home.

Vows: magic words, a spellcasting.

* * *

IN THE END, OF COURSE, Wanda must give Vision up. Dismantle the Hex and let go. She frees the town. Apologizes. Banishes herself to a remote cabin, where she meditates to try to understand how she erred. Her experience in Westview has revealed her to be the Scarlet Witch, a wielder of rare chaos magic. She wants to know what to do with this power. What to do differently, next time.

* * *

BEFORE SHUTTING THE DOOR forever on the place that had been my home, I left behind a journal composed of all the scraps I had written to and about the man of mist over the years. Diary entries. Poems. Texts I had wanted to save. I had typed and cut and pasted them as an engagement gift, years ago.

After everything exploded, I updated the journal with things I had written in the almost ten years since the initial gift was offered. More poems. More writing. A copy of my vows. I sat the journal, folded in its red and blue cover, on the empty shelf where my library had been. It laid there like a thick heart, bulging at the seams, its binding an artery-like stitch. It felt gory, like it should have oozed blood.

* * *

IN A FLASHBACK, Vision sits with Wanda and delivers what is arguably the show's heartbeat line. He asks whether grief could not be thought of as the love that endures after a loss. This is beautiful, luminous, a worthwhile question. It echoes through the show like golden sparks.

But what to do with love run through with grief *before* a loss? What to do with love built on illusion?

I could not locate us onscreen, except here. A couple rising in the air of their living room, exhausted and defeated.

* * *

I DREAM A NEW DREAM NOW. I reach for new images. I reach for new emotions.

The labyrinth shifts, the heart's collage kaleidoscopic. The flour and paint recede into fragments like stars retreating from day.

Scorched

Ekphrasis on *The Paper Bag Princess*

A few days after everything explodes, I go to the local bookstore and buy myself a copy of *The Paper Bag Princess*, written by Robert Munsch and illustrated by Michael Martchenko. My mother read me this book as a child. It was one of my favorite stories. It tells of Princess Elizabeth, who is betrothed to Prince Ronald, and how their castle is destroyed by a fearsome dragon, who carries Ronald off.

Elizabeth loses everything in the fire, including all of her elegant dresses. The only thing remaining is a dirty paper bag and her melted, damaged crown. Elizabeth makes a dress from the bag and goes to rescue Ronald.

Once at the dragon's lair, Elizabeth has to use her wits. She devises a plan to outsmart the dragon, knowing she cannot overpower him. The beast is enormous and ferocious. After she convinces him to demonstrate his abilities, he uses his fiery breath to burn down thirty forests. He flies around the world in ten seconds.

Following these feats, the dragon is exhausted. He falls into a deep slumber. Elizabeth enters the lair to rescue Ronald. But upon their reunion, Ronald berates her. He criticizes her paper bag dress. Her ash-scented, tangled hair.

In the end, Elizabeth dances off into the literal sunset, leaving Ronald and his judgments behind. According to the Edmonton Public Library, the book was challenged when it came out in the 1980s for allegedly going against family values. With the implication being that Elizabeth should have acquiesced to Ronald? Begged forgiveness for her messy hair?

When everything exploded, I bought this book because there were five images I needed to see. I remembered them vividly from childhood, but regardless, I needed to see them. And I didn't want to Google them. I wanted to hold them in my hands.

The first is of Elizabeth staring at Ronald with her hands clasped, hearts around her head. In this image, Ronald has his back to her. He holds a tennis racket. His facial expression is aloof.

The second is of Ronald being carried off. He looks helpless as the dragon smirks over his shoulder at Elizabeth standing in the wreckage. The castle is in ruin, smoke rising from the rubble. Elizabeth can only stare in shock.

The third is of Elizabeth getting angry. She wears her paper bag dress, follows the trail of horse bones the dragon leaves in his wake. She does not run away. She does not sit and cry. She buckles down. She makes do with what she has.

The fourth is of Ronald pointing accusingly at Elizabeth. His racket is still in his hand. She looks down, defensively, at her makeshift dress. The couple is surrounded by bones.

The final image is the one of the sunset. Elizabeth in silhouette, leaping toward the sky. He has shown his true colors, and so she is free. There is nothing holding her back.

This was how it felt, fighting the third party. The beast, ever-present, leaving a trail of bones. A tug-of-war. A shock, and then a bear-down.

I only wish I could say I defeated it. But some things do not work like that.

And in the story, even for the woman who does defeat her beast, only discouragement awaits. *Elizabeth* is at fault. *Elizabeth* is all wrong. *Elizabeth* should have known better.

In the end, Elizabeth does know better than to waste time. She takes her wits, her will to live. She leaves the desert barefoot. Leaves behind her smoldered crown. Dances toward better days.

Golden
Ekphrasis on "Electric" Music Video

It is after spending a week alone in the house, after he leaves, that I crack. The cavernous silence of the vacant home rolls me over its tongue. In the stillness of the night, I jump at every sound. I hate being alone, the driveway conspicuously empty, next to a neighbor a passerby once told me was a rapist. I sleep with the hall light on. I keep shoes by my bed. Pepper spray sits on the nightstand.

Abandonment is my biggest trigger. Abandonment, and shock.

* * *

WHEN HE FINALLY RETURNS, briefly, in person, it is because a package has arrived, too large for me to move with the chronic pain in my right shoulder. He enters through the door we painted together. From across the room, our eyes lock, live wires. The image that comes to mind is of severed power lines, sparking and writhing on wet pavement. Steam and plasma rising in the air.

He walks directly to the refrigerator. Pulls out and opens a beer. He cannot speak to me without doing that. He cannot speak to me.

* * *

WHEN WE CALL IT THE END, I am incandescent with sorrow, rage, and relief.

*   *   *

ON THE SEVENTH DAY, I drag myself to a socially distanced literary event, where I had been invited to read a story a few weeks earlier. The skies are dark; the wind is howling. I hold the edge of my billowing coat down with one hand and clutch my trembling pages in the other. The story, written months ago, tells of a girl made from clouds stepping out of a human woman's body. The cloud girl asks the human why she has allowed her spirit to become wet tinder. She brushes the woman's hair, making it grow and grow until it is yards long. She texts someone longed-for on the human's behalf. She knows what the human needs.

I did not see it for what it was. Did not see it as prophecy.

That night, I stay at a friend's house because reality feels like it is starting to unravel. I have barely slept in a week. Two hours here, three there. Eating feels impossible. I choke down two Ritz crackers with a teaspoon of peanut butter in the middle. It takes me fifteen minutes. I dry-heave into the sink at some point, coughing up bile. I feel I should not be alone.

My friend tucks me into lavender sheets, and a furious storm descends. When I return to the house the following morning, the power is out. This is too much. "I get it," I say to God. "I get it."

For the first time in my life, I buy a same-day ticket. To my mother's. I buy it one-way.

*   *   *

EVERYONE COMES to pick me up from the airport. Everyone. My mother, my stepfather, my brother, and his girlfriend. They all want to be there.

Because there is no center seatbelt in the back, my brother and his girlfriend say they will be my seatbelt. They sit on either side of me, hold hands across my waist. They literally bridge the gaping chasm in my belly, which feels like it is a black hole. They bridge it with their hands. With literal love. Their warm shoulders press against mine.

On the guest bed, they have piled nearly thirty stuffed animals. "To protect you," they say, and smile.

* * *

DAYS PASS. Now, I exist in limbo. I have not heard back from the job.

"Can I respond to what you said?" Cerulean asks on the phone, shortly after the video call where my years of repressed emotion came out.

I am staring at a rosebud in my mother's yard. It is golden, like a horizon at dawn. The other blooms have all crisped up. It is the only fresh flower on the bush. Dew adorns the fastened bud.

"Can I respond?" he quietly asks.

"Yes," I whisper. "Yes."

* * *

NOW THERE IS EVEN MORE riding on the job. It could be the paper dove that would carry me home, back to evergreens. Back to so much.

Days pass. Cerulean and I talk every night. Days pass. We talk. The sky glows orange.

* * *

IN THE MORNINGS, I fall into a ritual. I listen to "Golden" by Harry Styles and "Electric" by Katy Perry while putting on makeup in the mirror. It eases my nerves. Gives me somewhere to place my hope. The songs bristle with energy, and I want to ride the wave.

When I first applied for the job, I painted my toenails golden. The academic job market is ferocious, fierce. I had applied for ninety-eight full-time jobs over the years and been fortunate enough to be hired on full-time at the college

I had previously taught at as an adjunct professor while finishing my doctorate long-distance in the desert state. I loved the school, but I wanted to come home. And the teaching load was unsustainably large. Each year, I felt a bit weaker.

A few years prior, I had been a finalist for a job with a lighter load, near my west coast family, if not in my hometown. It had been my ninety-seventh try. I came in second. I felt a future rupture before me.

Now, this was my ninety-ninth attempt. And this was a true dream job. I prayed. I painted my toenails golden because I did not want to be silver. I did not want to come in second.

I listened to "Golden," willed golden energy into my cells. The song a pot of amber, of honey.

"Electric" came out the week everything exploded. A song about lightning and light. It was released to help celebrate *Pokémon*'s twenty-fifth anniversary. In the music video, a female Pikachu goes back in time to help out her younger self, Pichu. The two work in tandem to set the younger one on the right path.

After I finished my doctorate in 2016, I spent the summer writing pages of poems where the past and present met, where I was doubled. Helping my younger sister-self out. Having an older self help me. For this reason, and my affection for Pikachu, I was unexpectedly touched by the music video.

In this new job application limbo, I felt locked in a waiting room outside of time. Wanting to evolve into my next stage of life, to be the fruit of my younger self's efforts. Pleading with a future self to take my hand, already. Take my hand and lead me forward.

Golden. Electric. I look in the mirror. We wait. We wait. We wait.

* * *

I TELL MY MOTHER there is a rose motif winding through the brackets of my life. The single white rose in the yard that had been mine. The magenta rose protruding obstinately through fenceposts. The anomalous yellow rose in her garden. How they felt like symbols of hope.

She reaches into a cupboard and presents me with a bottle: a lotion scented like roses. I smear it on my body each morning, fresh from the shower. Pray. Sing. *Golden. Electric.*

*　*　*

IT IS THERE, standing before the bathroom mirror, where I receive the fateful email. *Pleased to inform you.* My eyes grow huge. The air smells like ten thousand roses.

I run up the stairs. They know without a word. They see joy wash over my face.

*　*　*

I HUG THEM EACH IN TURN. I have another one-way ticket. My next stop is my hometown. To visit the campus. To see Cerulean in person. We grin at each other and I pick up my backpack, ready to head to the car.

In the garden, by the gate, I pass by the rose bush. The yellow rose has opened, its petals sprawled wide. Its center is vibrant: fuchsia and magnificent. It looks like a held breath exhaled.

Pages and Feathers
Ekphrasis on *Tsubasa: Reservoir Chronicle*

In the manga *Tsubasa: Reservoir Chronicle*, a princess named Sakura follows her childhood friend Syaoran into a ruin and accidentally activates a magic seal stamped on the floor of one room. The spell causes a pair of enormous wings to appear behind the princess, who rises into the air. Then the ruin begins to crumble, and the wings dissipate, scattering feathers in every direction. Sakura falls, and when Syaoran catches her, she is unconscious and ice-cold.

Soon, it is revealed that the wings represented Sakura's memory—or her heart, as the manga puts it—and that pieces of it have drifted to various worlds across many dimensions. Syaoran and Sakura must travel together to find the feathers and restore the princess' memory. With each fragment that is found, her body grows a bit warmer. She becomes more herself. She comes back from the edge of death. When a feather is found, it is placed over her chest and absorbed there in ripples of light. The heart something watery, something disturbed.

This was what came to mind when I learned that a literary journal containing a poem of mine had arrived at my father's house. My mail was still being forwarded there; I had just moved into my new home. When he told me the journal had come, I took an Uber over at once. I did not want to wait for the bus. The journal beckoned to me like a beacon. I answered. I moved as if pulled.

My father had set it on the kitchen table. I tore off the plastic wrapper. I ran my hand over the journal's front cover. A feather. A piece of me back.

It was a poem I had written before everything exploded. It felt like a missive from a self who had died. Holding the journal felt like reaching across time and space, and taking her hand.

In my mind, with a ripple, the page fluttered into my chest. My body reclaimed some of its heat.

The Torch

O ne day, as I am writing this, a candle explodes. It is the candle I have lit faithfully, ritualistically, every time I work on this book. Each time I add pages. It was one of the last gifts the man of mist gave me. A candle from a small, independent business I liked. Many of their candles were named for Greek goddesses, and I had bought myself the Artemis one in the past, so I assume the one he has given me is Artemis again. I receive it as part of a birthday present two weeks before he walks out. When he does, I squeeze each of my hands with the other repeatedly and stare at the candle. I do not know what to do. In the end, I pack it with the rest of my tiny altar.

After I am settled in my new life—because I do not want to waste the candle—I decide to burn it as I write. But because it feels contaminated by his touch, I insulate it. I place it in an enormous white and gold mug my friend has made me. On it is an image of a quill and an ink pot. This feels like something that can contain the candle's associations. Make proximity feasible.

The candle burns down, inch by inch, as I write twenty pages, then forty. It is in March, the edge of spring, six months after I begin, that the wax grows so low, I can no longer see the flicker of the flame over the cup's edge as I work.

I am writing about the turning point: the part of this process where I feel there is more pain behind me than before me. The point where I feel more sutured than not. When I feel ready to stop bleeding out.

As my fingers hit keys, I notice small flecks in the air. *Bugs?* I wonder. I swat at them, but they remain. At last, I look at the candle and see a thin pillar of gray smoke. *No,* I realize. *Ash. It's ash.* Floating in the air of my home. The candles have dried leaves and stones embedded in them. Something must have caught flame, turned to soot.

I look in the cup and watch the fire blaze brightly, quite large. I take a breath and try to blow it out. I try three breaths. Each fails to quell it. I gaze around nervously. I want to put it out. More specks of ash drift in the air.

I pour a few drops of water from my bottle onto the fire, and it absolutely explodes. (I will later learn this is the worst way to put out a soy wax fire, that you are supposed to smother it, not wet it, but at the time, I do not know this.) The flame triples in size, shooting up at least six inches from the mouth of the cup. Red and gold and hot blue sparks shoot in all directions from the screeching column of fire. It hisses terribly, like a monster, like a snake. A demon hit with holy water. Liquid wax sprays in a foot-wide radius, 360 degrees. A circle of destruction. Paths of ash smear all over my desk. I stare in fascination and horror. The thought creeps through my mind in slow motion: *I hope my home does not burn down.*

After about ten seconds of this spectacle, the fire dims, then hushes. Droplets of wax harden all around me. My desk looks like someone has driven in miniature donuts with charcoal wheels, peeling out. The image of the vibrant scene is scorched into my mind. *A firework,* I think. *A fire fountain.*

This is when I dare to touch the candle. I pull its jar from inside the mug. I have not seen it uncloaked in months. My eyes widen. It is not Artemis, as I had assumed. It is named for the goddess Hecate.

The morning after the candle explodes, I blow my nose and ash comes out. Like my body had held a cremation.

* * *

I AM FAMILIAR WITH ARTEMIS, but less so with Hecate, so I research this goddess. I learn she is affiliated with magic, with crossroads, with the underworld. She accompanies Demeter on her quest to fetch Persephone after the girl is abducted to the land of the dead. In ancient carvings, Hecate carries a torch. Sometimes, she has three faces. She is considered neither all good nor all evil. She is considered multifaceted. Complex.

Because of this complexity—the symbolism ambiguous—I contemplate the meaning of the eruption for a week. On a visit, I ask my family about it. They close their eyes and concentrate. "It doesn't feel bad. Just *final*," my brother says. "Conclusive." My instinct says the same.

I return home, and as I continue to turn the riddle over in my mind, I am sitting beside the wreckage of wax one morning and I all but see Hecate, dripping in a veil of stars, lean in and whisper in my ear. *Do you think exorcisms are supposed to be pretty?* I all but hear her laugh. Not cruel. Not taunting. Just honest. Just, *Well? Really—do you?*

I stare at the soot marks. I suppose they are not. Pretty. I suppose it is not pretty.

This cauterizing wounds. This sucking out the venom. This gruesome, wincing crawl away from pain.

I suppose it is not pretty. This opening the chest to the fire that burns away infection. Relinquishing dead cells to let new ones grow. The agony that gets called healing.

The Ruby's Song

Ekphrasis on *The Blue Beard Picture Book,*
Through the Woods, and *Speak: The Graphic Novel*

During my three months spent couch-surfing, I visit a friend in New Jersey. For three days, I wander her garden, learn the names of various mushrooms, swim with her and her children in the nearby lake. It is a respite. In photos, I smile genuinely. But beneath these grins, there is also a void. An abyss I work to keep at bay.

At the visit's end, my friend drops me off at an outdoor train stop, where I wait to catch a ride back to the airport. The sun is vividly, aggressively bright. Foliage shines all around us. It is a train stop far from town. We are enveloped by summer, by green.

The train pulls up, and I hug my friend goodbye. I am smiling. I am grateful to have seen her. I roll my bag along the aisle until I find a seat. Now, for the next few hours, I am alone.

The train moves quickly, and I keep my eyes forward after observing that the scenery outside the window does not change much. It is all fresh leaves, lit by the August sun.

I keep my eyes forward as we speed by the woods. Branches crisscrossing, chaotic streaks and blurs. They resemble a painter's hectic brushstrokes. In my mind's eye, abruptly, there appears the rough sketch of a body, bruised and bloodied, lying silent on the ground among pine needles, hidden in the woods. I see this only in my mind's peripheral vision. I keep my eyes forward. I will not look at it yet.

I cannot look at it, yet.

* * *

I WILL SAY in therapy a few weeks later, thinking of this memory, "I feel like I'm carrying a corpse in my arms. The corpse of the girl I was in the desert state. I feel like she was killed and left in the woods. I have to clean the body, dress the body. I have to give her a funeral. But I'm not sure how."

I know it is up to me. No one else will do it.

No one else *can* do it.

* * *

ONCE, WHEN I ENDED a relationship, the man said to me, "All right. But let's have a funeral for our time together. We need to honor it."

He brought out a bottle of whiskey, and we toasted. We took turns toasting good things. Things we were grateful for, though we accepted it was time to part ways. Trying to lay this chapter of our lives to rest respectfully. With some reverence.

Together, we buried the chapter in the ground. Marked the grave with flowers of words. Stood and bowed our heads together, sent it on its way.

* * *

THERE WAS NOTHING like that, this time. Nothing to honor the end of a marriage. It was cutting. Emotionally violent.

As I watch the green smear of the trees whir past, I know it must be me who provides it. I must be the one who cleanses the body. Only then can I set down its weight.

* * *

FOR YEARS, in graduate school, I was obsessed with fairy tale retellings. Ones that gave greater agency to the female characters in them. I read them, wrote them, breathed them for months. Something in this felt necessary. Healing.

I wrote about Rapunzel, Snow White, Sleeping Beauty, Rose Red, Cinderella, and Gretel. I wrote about Little Red Riding Hood, the Little Mermaid, the Snow Queen, Beauty, Vasilisa, Odette, and Tinker Bell. I wrote of the nameless women who spin straw into gold, detect a pea beneath a stack of mattresses, ask a magic fish for power. After thoroughly exploring the stories I was raised on, I sought out ones unfamiliar to me: The Sea-Hare, The Goose Girl, The Six Swans.

Never in this time, though it was a tale I knew well, did I write about the story of Bluebeard.

I wonder, now, why. The omission was not deliberate. It mysteriously slipped through my grip.

Too close to home, perhaps. A groom with a roomful of secrets, of harm. A bride with the key in her hand. The two of them prowling their castle alone, cold and suspicious and aloof.

In Charles Perrault's version of the story, the bride's brothers come to save her. In Angela Carter's, it is the mother. For after she has unlocked the forbidden door, Bluebeard condemns the girl to death.

In all the versions I have read, the bride survives. In some, she buries the collection of Bluebeard's dead wives that line the walls of the secret room. In some, she falls in love again. In some, she even remarries.

I was not looking to be in this story. Maybe that's what hid it from my sight. I did not want to be the woman in the doorway, smothering a gasp with her hand.

*   *   *

IN THE WAY these things so often go, it was a ruby in the ring he gave me. In Carter's telling, it is a ruby choker that Bluebeard presents to his bride.

A Walter Crane illustration in *The Blue Beard Picture Book* shows the wife on her knees, pleading with Bluebeard for mercy. The husband, clad all in opulent red, scowls coldly down.

* * *

EMILY CARROLL'S COLLECTION of horror comics, *Through the Woods*, has a Bluebeard-inspired story too. A young bride discovers the body of a killed wife in the floorboards of the groom's stately manor.

This bride, too, receives a choker of rubies. Carroll said in an interview that she had not read Carter's story. The gem, it seems, offers itself up in these tales. Like a warning light, a sun-stained bulb of oxygen rising through the depths of a lake.

* * *

DURING GRADUATE SCHOOL, I wrote a paper on Carroll's illustrations in the graphic novel adaptation of Laurie Halse Anderson's *Speak*. The book is a collaboration: Anderson herself adapted the text, and Carroll drew the illustrations. In my paper, I explored my fascination with Halse's decision to work with a famous horror artist. When I read *Speak*, I was of course horrified by the sexual assault that dwells at the center of the text (silenced, hidden, kept in the throat of the protagonist for far too long), but I did not read it as a "horror novel," categorically. Carroll's illustrations shed new light on the text, made me realize that yes, it *is* a horror novel. Horror is the rightful genre. As a survivor myself (years ago, long before I was married), I should not have needed to be told this.

Perhaps it is an issue of genre itself. What stories get classified as "problem novels," what stories get classified as "horror."

In recent years, I have said this to friends, reading of political events: "It feels like a horror story." For many, I know, it has always been this way. I wonder: the genre of our country.

* * *

I DID NOT WANT to be in a horror story. Did not ask for this body in the woods. Maybe this is part of what felt so isolating: his genre never matched up with mine. Our soundtracks never synced.

I read once that people, consciously or not, assign a genre to the story of their life. How memory itself is so inclined toward story—ask almost anyone, and they will tell you of a crossroads that altered the course of their lives. Sometimes the difference between a moment that broke them and a moment that only *nearly* broke them is the telling. The story. What came next.

A friend once asked me to repeat something I said in a workshop, so I did: "I think the job of therapy is to help you tell your story in a way that makes sense to you."

Maybe this is writing's job, too.

* * *

I HAVE ALWAYS BEEN drawn to stories of adventure—magic and drama and questing. Monsters to face and deep bonds to forge. Stories with romance and danger and characters who find determination in the bleakest, bleakest times.

Maybe that is what I got—what I am getting—in the end. Maybe I did not despair, watching those stories, because I trusted the genre. I knew what would come next was not a tragedy.

So at least for my own life, I can say with some conviction: trust me, this is not a tragedy.

* * *

I DON'T KNOW what his genre was. I don't know what story he is telling with his life.

* * *

IN *SPEAK: THE GRAPHIC NOVEL*, there are many images of trees. The protagonist, Melinda, draws the word "tree" from a container of many possible words at the start of her school year in art class. The teacher tells the students they will make art about whatever word they drew for the whole year. Melinda's initial boredom eventually yields deeper layers of trauma: her assault took place beneath a tree.

As the year goes on, she stares down her horror and approaches the theme from new angles. In the end, she exits her personal woods. "I survived," she thinks. "I'm here." In this panel, Carroll draws Melinda's hand outstretched, touching the trunk of the tree. The claw-like branches from the book's earlier pages give way to smoother ones with leaves.

* * *

THE TRAIN SPEEDS ON. We exit the woods. I carry the body with me. I am not afraid to clean its ruby wounds. My throat unlocked to sing its eulogy.

Ascent
Ekphrasis on *Gris*

In *Gris*, a platformer and puzzle video game, grief forms a literal landscape. Players move through the world as a young girl who must navigate five environments corresponding to the stages of grief as theorized by Elisabeth Kübler-Ross, confronting the terrors and riddles therein.

In the last level, the girl regains her voice, which she lost in the game's opening scene. Having fallen—deep, deep into a canyon where relentless winds blow, deeper still into a labyrinthine forest, deeper still to the very bottom of the ocean—it is her voice that allows her to climb. When you press the button prompting her to sing, dormant flowers blossom and metal birds' wings spread, providing the girl with the platforms she needs to make her ascent back upward. It is the final, vital ability she gains.

I think of my playlist, *what it was like.* The theme that emerged, of breathlessness.

It is the voice, the song, that opens the way. The voice that unfurls the path.

Containers
Ekphrasis on *Final Fantasy X*

Cerulean and I get the keys to our new home two days before orientation for my new job starts. Eight days before department meetings start. Sixteen before the first day of classes. I have only the suitcase I have been living out of all summer. The moving pod containing the rest of my things has been delayed, rerouted out of state.

We have a mattress, a bedspread, and a new set of sheets. A few cups, plates, and utensils. He has been living with his parents, and his belongings, up to this point, have been relatively few. We are essentially starting from scratch.

Slowly, over the next few months, we will acquire new things together. We will pick curtains, paintings, a coffee table. But for now, we eat dinner with plates balanced on our laps, or standing over the kitchen sink.

I have two weeks to build a stable foundation from which to launch, to teach. Two weeks to put a professor together from the smoking jigsaw puzzle in my hands.

* * *

I THINK ABOUT what my heroes would do. I remember my young self trying to pick a major at age eighteen, nineteen, twenty. How I said I wanted to study "what it means to be human." How I finally settled on literature.

What was it all for, if not this? What was all that studying for? Why examine the heart so closely, if not to navigate crisis?

Four months later, in class, we will be studying Aristotle's ideas about catharsis and these words will come out of my mouth, unplanned: "There are some things nothing can prepare you for. But literature can try."

* * *

MY FRIEND ONCE SAID writing is the process of trying to be "the most yourself." Trying to figure out who you are and being "the most that self." I think about this a lot. I think stories can help guide the way. How seeing something in a story that resonates with you can illuminate something in yourself.

I think often, too, about Keats' idea of *Soul-making*. How maybe souls are added to instead of discovered or excavated. Maybe this is how it works: we make ourselves, choice by choice.

* * *

WHEN THE POD FINALLY ARRIVES—five days before classes start—a fire ignites in my chest. I stride through the parking lot, key in hand.

The first thing I take out is the blanket I saved, the one my grandmother made me, the one Cerulean and I cuddled under as teenagers, the one I used on my bed, but only when I was alone, from time to time in the desert state.

A woman waves me down as I walk back to the building. "I can tell that's important to you," she says, taking a drag from her cigarette.

"It is," I nod. My arms are full. The quilt drapes down like gossamer wings.

* * *

THE SECOND THING I take out is my writing desk. The 3x1' wood antique that was my office, classroom, and writing space for the first fourteen months of the pandemic. I wrote a poetry book there, years ago. The desk was a gift I gave to myself. It was my attempt to take up space, to offer writing a landing spot.

Now, it has an enormous crack down the middle. One that was not there before. The man of mist had loaded it in precariously, insistently, when I was not there, despite me asking him not to. The flame inside my chest billows.

I take the desk, which he had said I was too weak to move, in both hands and lug it up the stairway. *It's still here. It's still mine.* These thoughts loop in my mind. *It's still here. It's still mine.*

I'm still here.

* * *

I WRITE AT A larger desk now. Cerulean was emphatic. "You deserve more space. You need more space to do your work."

I appreciate this. Still, the old desk I kept. "We're trauma-bonded," I say.

The crack in its face a long scar, a reminder. Its presence reassuring. It lived.

* * *

THREE DAYS BEFORE classes start, I open a box and pull out my plastic figurines. They have traveled with me from home to grad school to more grad school to the desert state, and now back home. I have carried them with me as visible emblems of the person I want to be. Brave. True. Kind and accepting. I have set them on shelves in four states. Sailor Venus and Chibi Moon dolls from my mother, cherished since childhood. A small statue of Yuna, a character from *Final Fantasy X*—my favorite character from the game. Her quiet strength and discipline inspired me as I completed my dissertation, nearly two thousand miles from my advisor, my friends, the university library. Struggling against the tide, trying to save the drowning marriage. Struggling in good faith for what I thought was love.

Yuna's neck is horribly bent. Her gaze has literally been shoved downward by the angle she was hurriedly packed in, the journey she has made. She looks crestfallen. Defeated.

"Oh," I murmur. "Poor Yuna."

Cerulean knows who she is. He was there when the game came out. We played it together. He picks the figure up.

Later, I hear him blow-drying something. He runs the hairdryer over Yuna's mangled neck until it becomes pliable. He straightens it. Raises her gaze.

I do not know how I am so lucky.

* * *

AFTER I HAUL OUT the writing desk and a few other heavy items, my father calls, asking if he can come over and help unpack the pod. The fire in me is raging. At first, I refuse.

"I want to do it myself," I fume. "To show him what I can do."

My father pauses, then says, "Those are ghosts whispering in your ear. Who wins if you listen? Don't let the ghosts win."

The fire is raging, but I consider this. Earlier, I had received a text from Cerulean at work, asking how things were going.

"I'm bathing in the blood of my past," I had answered, only half-joking.

"That's awesome," he says. "Have you eaten?"

Now, on the phone with my father, I consider my sweat, my growling stomach, the chronic pain in my shoulder. I consider the tendon it takes so little to aggravate, the one that sends pain upward into my skull, catalyzing ocular migraines that turn the vision in my right eye to static.

"Okay," I mutter. "I could really use your help." I humble myself. I say, "Thank you."

I yield. I wrangle my roaring pride. I do not let the ghosts win.

* * *

IN *FINAL FANTASY X*, Yuna is not just a summoner—a warrior who can make pacts with mystical creatures who come to her aid during battle—she is also an exorcist. Beckoning and repelling energy as needed. Tidal. A rhythmic flow of breath.

In a ritual called The Sending, Yuna ushers the souls of those killed in battle on to the afterlife. If a summoner does not do this, souls tethered to the mortal plane by resentment risk turning into monsters and haunting the living with malice.

In The Sending, Yuna steps onto the ocean, bare feet placed upon the waves. She moves out across the brine and sways her staff, twirls in a kind of slow dance. A pillar of water rises beneath her, lifting her into the air. From here, she coaxes the errant souls onward. Depicted as tiny floating orbs, they soar off into the sky.

On the shore, people weep and fall to their knees. But they know this needs to be done. The Sending is funereal. A ritual of grief. A ritual that also honors life.

Yuna does this solemnly. She takes her duty seriously. She moves along—transforms—pain.

* * *

ONE PIECE OF FURNITURE emerged from the pod that had been in my family for years. Like the figurines, it had moved to many places as I studied, worked, and wrote.

In the desert state, it had sat in the bedroom. A dark wooden bureau with an oval mirror. Given the memories stuffed in every drawer, I had been reluctant to bring it. Now, seeing it stand in my new home, a shudder runs through me. A tremor.

Cerulean is very good at dispelling things like this without really trying—diffusing situations where my own anxiety might reach out and snatch me by the throat. When, two days before classes start, we buy a colander sturdier than the flimsy one I had brought with me, I ask what we should do with the old one. I am holding the colander by its plastic handle, memories swimming and dripping through the grate.

Cerulean shrugs and takes it, puts it on his head, and keeps putting silverware away.

The object is instantly neutralized.

A quiet exorcism.

* * *

I FOLLOW HIS LEAD. I take the statue of Yuna and place it on top of the dresser. *To purify it,* I think, setting her down. We add other objects that bring delight. A stuffed Totoro. A comic book. A pin Cerulean got me of baby Pichu lifting weights.

I hear echoes: *Golden. Electric.*

Like this, we suck the venom out. Like this, we send the ghosts away.

Radiance

Ekphrasis on *X-Men*

I am fourteen when *X-Men* hits theaters. I am young and looking for role models everywhere. Much about the movie makes an impression on me—specifically, how characters' powers often seem to both correspond to and shape their personalities—but what dazzles me most is a scene near the end featuring Storm, a woman with the power to control weather.

In this scene, the heroes Storm, Jean Grey, and Cyclops are fighting Toad, an enemy who can leap enormous heights, spit projectiles of goo, and use his long tongue as a weapon. Toad quickly gains the upper hand, incapacitating Jean Grey and Cyclops and kicking Storm down an elevator shaft. To most, this would be a death sentence. But as he moves to the roof to make his escape, the elevator doors behind him start to rattle and glow. He turns around, confused. The doors open and there is Storm. Levitating. Surging with lightning. Her silver hair swirls around her face. Her eyes flash white, twin moons.

Storm's expression is serene, but she also brims with confidence. She summons down lightning and thunder and wind, sending her foe flying into New York Harbor. When she has finished, she turns on her heel, radiant and undisturbed.

I want to learn from this. A woman soaring up the walls of the pit that was meant to be her end. Shining with blue light and crackling awe. Serenely, defiantly alive.

With Fists Aglow

Ekphrasis on *Captain Marvel*

In the desert state, my sense of truth about myself and the world is challenged repeatedly. It is only with some distance that I realize this. Start to untangle the narrative.

* * *

NEAR THE BEGINNING of *Captain Marvel,* extraterrestrial commander Yon-Rogg tells his trainee Vers that her emotions can endanger her in battle.

He tells her doubt and anger are weaknesses. Orders her to keep herself in check.

Vers suffers memory loss. She cannot remember anything prior to six years ago, when she was found by the Kree army and taken into their ranks. A small metallic circle on the side of her neck grants her powers, or so she is told. She can shoot energy beams from her hands. But as the leader of the Kree—an entity known only as the Supreme Intelligence—warns, it is a gift that can be revoked.

Occasionally, Vers catches glimpses of a previous life, a life before the army, in dreams. She is told to ignore these, to let them go. She is told she is alone in the universe, that she should be grateful to serve as a Kree soldier. The Supreme Intelligence chastises her, telling her how weak she is, how worthless. How it is only through the grace of the Kree that Vers' life means anything. For a long time, Vers believes this.

Eventually, she finds hard evidence that she led a prior life on Earth. But when she asks Yon-Rogg about it, he snaps at her, tells her to stop being so emotional. He tells her to use her head. To be rational.

She is gaslit, gaslit, gaslit. Made to believe she is wrong.

* * *

"I'M NOT WRONG," I once cried, in the desert state. "I'm not wrong. Please, stop scoffing at me."

Applying for the new job felt like reaching for something. Reaching. A pinprick of light.

* * *

AT ONE POINT, VERS—who has uncovered her true name, Carol Danvers—confronts the Supreme Intelligence. She has learned the Kree do *not* supply her powers. Her powers have been within her for years. She realizes she has been fighting at only partial capacity, in fact. She plucks the metallic circle from her neck, which it turns out is a dampener, suppressing her potential. She wonders aloud what will happen when she is free.

Gold light spills through her body, surrounds her. She rises into the air.

* * *

I AM TOLD TO BE grateful for my job in the desert state, despite a teaching load that is recognized as unsustainable in several industry think pieces. Despite its leadership receiving a no-confidence vote. Despite the way I come home crying.

Meanwhile, local lawmakers do the things repressive lawmakers do: try to ban discussion of racism in schools, try to ban books about gender identity, try to tell women they belong nowhere but inside the home. I cry. I am too emotional, I am told.

I am told I cannot possibly experience gender or sexuality on a spectrum despite having had feelings for women, despite having kissed women, despite feeling a twinge of elation in my chest watching *Revolutionary Girl Utena* as a teen, with its protagonist who explores expansive ideas about gender all the time.

I am told I am antisocial because I am an introvert. I am told something is wrong with me for pursuing advanced degrees.

When I bristle at a baseball game, flinching as a stranger sloshes beer onto my foot and launching into a rapid-fire explanation, Cerulean tilts his head, studies me, and says, "Oh, I see. You've had to defend yourself almost...*existentially*, haven't you?"

I freeze. The word echoes. Yes. I have. Yes. Existentially.

* * *

THE FINAL SHOWDOWN of the film is between Yon-Rogg and Carol, who stride toward each other in the desert. Even after so many lies have been exposed—indeed, perhaps, *because* they have been—Yon-Rogg resorts to manipulation.

He smirks at Carol, asking if she can face him without being ruled by her emotions.

He tells her to turn off her luminous power. He mocks it, scoffing and berating her. But mid-taunt, his speech is cut off: Carol fist-beams him into a rock.

She walks and stands over him, back against the sun. She is lit, brightly, from behind.

Calmly, matter-of-factly, Carol says she does not have to prove herself to him.

* * *

WHAT DO WE PROMISE, when we make a marriage vow? What might we promise if we break it?

What vows do we make to ourselves in this life? What happens if two vows conflict?

* * *

THE ENDING OF *Captain Marvel* is divisive. Some find the showdown anticlimactic. Some find it deeply moving.

For me, to see a woman stand up for herself and speak back against her brainwashing was medicinal. Carol learns her emotions are what give her strength. Her gut, her intuition, her pursuit of the truth. Her courage to not deny these things.

She does not have to prove herself. She shines in her knowledge. Aura radiating, aglow.

The Woman in the Bright Orange Dress
Ekphrasis on *Flaming June*

In thinking about devaluation, I always recall the painting *Flaming June*. Created by Sir Frederic Leighton in 1895, it depicts a woman sleeping in a brilliant orange dress. In the background is a glittering sea. Nowadays, it is an iconic image, one that enjoys international fame. But before that, it vanished for close to three decades and allegedly was once thought worthless.

Records of the painting's whereabouts drop off in the 1930s, only for the piece to reemerge in the 1960s, when Victorian-era art had fallen out of fashion. There is some debate as to how exactly the painting was rediscovered, but one popular story states that it was found boxed away in the chimney of a house in England, then sold at a thrift shop for a mere £60.

It was finally purchased by an art dealer, and soon caught the eye of Luis A. Ferré, a soon-to-be-governor of Puerto Rico who was, at the time, working to establish a new museum. Nowadays, the painting draws viewers to that museum constantly. It is considered by many to be a masterpiece.

When I read this story, I thought of every woman I know who has ever been devalued. Glorious in their vibrant auras, being told to sit still in a chimney. I thought of everyone I know who has ever had a bully. Someone who made them feel small.

I am grateful that *Flaming June* returned from that chimney. I'm grateful she found her new home. I'm grateful she can see just how loveable she is. That her brightest colors can shine.

Flight

In preparing my research talk and teaching demonstration for the job interview, I noticed that the materials drew from many parts of myself. There were things sourced from childhood, like my interest in mythology. Things from adolescence, like my interest in anime and manga. Things from undergrad, like reading literature through a postcolonial lens. Ideas about gender and sexuality from grad school. I drew from books I had read on my own as well as ones taught in school. I drew from my dissertation and my MFA thesis. It was a synthesis unlike anything I had done before. In past job interviews, I had emphasized different sides of myself, depending on what the role called for. In this case, I felt balanced—like I was showing up equally as a teacher, researcher, and artist.

This kind of synthesis that pulled from so many aspects of my training—formal and informal, analytic and creative—brought to mind an image of crafting a custom sword or vehicle. I felt like a blacksmith poring over different scraps, different metals. Bits of ore lay scattered on a table. I heated and fused them together. What resulted was chimeric: part academic, part intuitive. Part girl taking pages of notes in classrooms, part daydreamer gazing out the window. I had never made anything like it. It felt risky, experimental. I wasn't sure it would work. But it felt authentic, and like something I could not have made any sooner. Something that took every experience up to that point.

You know those scenes in movies where the spaceship or plane is hurtling off the cliff, and then it flies at the last second, inches from hitting the ground? It's a familiar scene, one I often found unrealistic. Like, really? The last second? That's when it finally works?

But this was how it felt: like the patchwork machine worked at the last possible second. Like I was pushed from a cliff, and my machine and I fell. And then, at the last second, we flew. When the personal stakes could not have been higher, the engine thrummed to life.

* * *

THE OTHER IMAGE that came to me repeatedly during the six-month process from the initial application to receiving the job offer was that of an enormous dragon, tethered down, slowly breaking her ropes. When I first saw the job ad, questions crossed my mind.

Your house: are you willing to give that up? Yes. In my mind, a tether stretched and snapped.

Your garden, too? You like growing mint plants. Yes. Muscles flexed; a taut rope frayed.

It went on like this, the image coming unbidden as the months crawled slowly along.

The day the yes came, my mind's eye showed the dragon shaking off her final binding, roaring against the buttercup sun, lifting into the sky.

In short: something struggled. Something flew.

The Right Words
Ekphrasis on *Alice 19th*

In the manga *Alice 19th*, words have the power to physically alter the fabric of reality. A group of young heroes has the power of Lotis Words, runes with supernatural abilities that can be invoked either by uttering the rune's name, like *rangu*, or by speaking words that correspond with the sentiment behind it, like courage. When the protagonist Alice runs into the street to save a rabbit, crying that she cannot ignore it, rangu is called upon, awakening her magic.

Throughout the series, characters invoke runes standing for love, protection, healing, and so on. They do this by uttering prayers, standing up for their beliefs, or telling difficult truths. Sometimes, the words work. Antagonists—often peers or family members whose pain has been exploited by the enemy—pause, calm down, come back to themselves. Wicked spells are broken when the needed words are heard. *I love you. I care for you. I'm sorry.*

Reading this manga as a girl, I put faith in this idea with my whole heart. I observed the way sincerity and vulnerability could work wonders. I thought, *Aren't the Lotis Words what many people are secretly longing to hear when their claws and fangs are out? Doesn't much aggression come from feeling isolated? Desperate and misunderstood?* In my twenties, I took classes on nonviolent communication, studied how to speak and react from a place of love.

I have seen the effects of Lotis Words in real life. Have been on both sides of this. I have seen eyes well at an overdue apology; have been the one whose eyes well, too. I have seen shoulders soften when the reminder comes: *I'm listening. I hear you. You're important to me.*

* * *

BUT IN THE FACE of the explosion, the Lotis Words failed. They shattered like shells against rock. I had faith that one of them—that something—would work. But nothing, none of them did.

Embrace
Ekphrasis on *Fruits Basket*

*W*ere is the line between compassion and self-erasure?
    I keep searching. I keep inquiring.
    What does justice look like? What does healing look like? What is the appropriate response?

"Where is your anger?" my therapist asks. "Get angry. You should be angry."

"I understand if you are angry," the man of mist once said to me.

"My anger is compartmentalized," I said to him, calm as a brook. My hands were folded on the table.

"Oh," he scoffed. "In a box I'll have to carry?" He had placed some boxes in my moving pod on my last day there. He had done it while I was staying at a friend's, had insisted on not accepting help.

He glared at me. I fell silent. I arranged my lips into a smile.

* * *

TURN THE OTHER CHEEK, I thought. *Don't fight back. It's too much trouble. More trouble than it's worth.*

I remember playing with a neighborhood boy when I was young. Five, or maybe six. I was swinging on the swing set in his yard when abruptly, grinning, he uncoiled the garden hose and turned it on, full blast. He aimed it at me. He was laughing. I smiled. It was freezing. I felt awful, embarrassed, confused. But I did not know how to articulate this. To shout it felt like letting him win. Water gushed into my ears, my eyes. Eventually, I hopped off the swing, still smiling. Pretending I was in on the game.

You might read this and think, *She has no survival instincts.* But this is a survival instinct, too.

* * *

FIGHT OR FLIGHT, the saying goes. But psychologists now recognize two other responses: freeze and fawn. I have been such a fawner, I may as well have spots. I fawn and fawn and fawn.

* * *

OFTEN—QUITE OFTEN—during my marriage, I thought about a scene I had watched as a teenager, one from the final episode of an anime called *Fruits Basket*. In it, a boy who has been possessed by a vengeful spirit takes on its form, becomes monstrous. He changes from a boy into something that looks like a gray, hairless rabbit. He is enormous, with huge, purple eyes.

The boy has had this ability for years. But he keeps it in check. Until he can't.

Fleeing from his loved ones, he hides in a forest by a lake. He is disgusted with himself.

The heroine, Tohru, does not have magic powers. But she goes to the lake, stumbling in shock, horrified by what she has seen, but determined. She goes to the monster and holds out her arms. She embraces him. He comes back to himself.

He is grateful. So grateful. Her love transforms him. It literally banishes a demon.

I was enchanted by this story. I took it in, absorbed it.

A gorgeous fantasy.

* * *

I WANTED TO BE THAT PURE. That accepting. I wanted to cure all the ills.

Starting at age twelve, I saved up for thick books on therapy. I listened to friends, often boys, online, who struggled with rage and despair. I thought I could help. I thought love would solve everything. I thought I could take it all on.

I see now that although love can accomplish many things, "everything" encompasses a lot.

And that perhaps this was part of a larger cultural narrative, one that can funnel people, often girls, into offering their veins as food.

And that offering your veins as food to certain beings can mean having your blood sucked right out.

Turning the other cheek does not always work. Fawning does not always mean survival.

*   *   *

I LIKE MANY ASPECTS of *Fruits Basket* still. I think in many cases, it works. The empathy works. Compassion works wonders. It's just that it's not failproof.

What determines it, perhaps, is the reciprocation. It has to flow both ways.

In the show, it does. The boy holds Tohru back. Maybe that's what makes the difference.

*   *   *

WHERE IS THE LINE between compassion and self-erasure? What recourse when the monster attacks you instead? How do you keep your soft heart intact while not letting your blood be sucked dry?

Flowing Water
Ekphrasis on *Adorned by Chi*

I find answers, as I so often do, in stories. They point me forward, toward healing.

*   *   *

IN *ADORNED BY CHI*, a comic written by Jacque Aye and illustrated by Magus Ato and Tiana Mone'e, a character named Kaira is a water magic user. She wields her power as compassionately as she can. As consciously as she can.

Kaira meditates, does yoga, and is a longtime vegetarian. She is inclined toward peaceful problem-solving. But when a monster called a Mmanwu attacks her friend Adaeze, she leaps into action. She transforms into magical girl form and gives the monster a warning.

When the Mmanwu insists on conflict, Kaira steels herself. She says she does not want to fight, that life has inherent value. But, she says, she cannot stand by while injustice is meted out.

Her eyes glow and she casts a water spell. The monster is vanquished. But instead of celebrating, Kaira weeps. She kneels and clasps her hands.

She prays for the Mmanwu, prays over its life. But she also stands by her conviction.

Kaira makes me contemplate questions about justice. And I understand: the answers are complex.

The questions are about when and how to stand up for what is right. When to push back instead of being passive, or fawning, or turning the other cheek.

* * *

I OFFERED HIM so many olive branches, I almost chopped down the whole tree. I would have chopped down the whole tree had he asked. Would have set fire to its leaves.

Instead, I douse the flame with water. I throw the ash into the sea.

I gather a bucket of cool rainwater and scatter it on the tree's roots.

Freezing Water

Ekphrasis on *Avatar: The Last Airbender* and *The Wheel of Time*

In *Avatar: The Last Airbender,* a character named Katara is a water magic user too. In the world of the animated show, her ability is called waterbending. Katara can manipulate water found in rivers and oceans with her hands—making it crash in waves, change states of matter, and sharpen into dagger-like prongs. As her journey progresses, her abilities grow. Once, in a pinch, when no apparent water is nearby, she realizes she can use her own sweat to waterbend and free herself from a cage. She is resourceful and inventive, with a strong sense of justice. She always tries to do what is right.

In one episode, an elderly woman named Hama offers to help Katara hone her waterbending. She teaches Katara how to suck the moisture out of trees and flowers. As a patch of lilies around the women wilts, Katara expresses sadness for them. Hama dismisses her concern, irritated. She says the end justifies the means.

Eventually, Hama reveals her disturbing secret: an art she has crafted called bloodbending. Using the water in the human body, she can control people's movements, using them as living puppets.

127

Katara is horrified. She says she has no desire for that power.

But Hama insists. She explains she developed bloodbending as a prisoner of the Fire Nation, who tried to wipe out her tribe. She used it on rats, then worked her way up until she took control of a guard's limbs and made him unlock her cell.

Now, she uses her ability to kidnap people from the Fire Nation, while masquerading as a kindly innkeeper. When Katara realizes that a string of disappearances has been caused by Hama herself, the two clash. In the end, Katara must resort to bloodbending to save her friends. Though Hama is captured, she mutters her snide congratulations.

Katara weeps, knowing she has claimed a power she cannot put back.

Later in the series, Katara has a chance to take revenge on the Fire Nation soldier who killed her mother. When she finds the man she thinks is him, she does it: she uses bloodbending. She forces him onto the ground, asking if he remembers who she is. When she realizes he is not the man she seeks, she turns away angrily, tears in her eyes.

Finally, she finds her mother's killer, Yon Rha. It is a rainy day, so Katara has plenty of water to work with. She attacks him on a muddy road, suspending daggers of ice inches from his face. But as he begs for his life, suggesting she kill his mother instead—to balance the scales, he perversely suggests—she realizes that he is pathetic. That hurting him will not bring her the peace she seeks.

She states, in the end, she has not forgiven Yon Rha. But she does not want his blood on her hands.

She asserts herself in a way that balances both her dignity and her code of honor.

* * *

I WRITE IN A MESSAGE once (only once), "The way you treated me was not okay."

It wasn't okay. But my wish is for healing.

This, perhaps, is a tiny water spell.

* * *

THINKING BACK on *Demon Slayer*, Cerulean suggests the term "emotionally intact" to distinguish between Tanjiro and Shinobu. Both have had trauma. Both have lost family. Both have been terribly wronged. But Tanjiro keeps his compassion.

This is the case, too, with Katara and Hama. Both have suffered tremendously. But one turns to vengeance, while the other does something else. She chooses another form of justice.

In the fantasy drama *The Wheel of Time*, a character named Ila who has similarly experienced unthinkable trauma says, "What greater revenge against violence than peace? What greater revenge against death than life?" She calls this the Way of the Leaf.

* * *

I WATCH KATARA'S SCENE over and over, asking how she makes her decision. In the end, it seems to me, she chooses her own spirit. The integrity of her own spirit.

* * *

THIS IS THE GOAL. Emotional intactness. Purification, not death.

Parting Water
Ekphrasis on *Moana* and *Spirited Away*

In *Moana*, an animated film from Disney, a young woman named Moana is charged with reviving the heart of an ancient goddess known as Te Fiti. The heart takes the shape of a small, green gem that can fit in the palm of Moana's hand. It has a spiral engraving on the front.

On her journey, Moana encounters a fiery deity called Te Kā, a giant made of burning rock and lava. Te Kā screeches horribly, hurtles enormous boulders and fireballs at Moana. In their first meeting, Moana is defeated; she must regather herself and return for a second attack.

But as Moana gazes at the being, she notices something. The spiral on the heart of Te Fiti is similar to the one on Te Kā's chest. In fact, there is a tiny notch in Te Kā's chest, the same size as the heart.

Moana turns to the ocean, who has been her wordless ally. Throughout the film, the ocean has arisen in sentient waves to scoop the girl up, carry her, and help her on her quest. Moana tells the sea to allow Te Kā to approach her.

The waters part, and Te Kā is temporarily transfixed by the sight of the heart glittering in the light. But then she starts charging toward Moana, pulling herself along across the wet sand.

Moana sings softly that she knows Te Kā's true name.

Te Kā slows and shuts her eyes, relieved. Moana places the green gem in the slot on the being's chest. Te Kā shakes off her lava coating, revealing the grassy and floral body of Te Fiti.

It is knowing the name that does it. Seeing the truth and naming it. Te Kā is also Te Fiti. Knowing the name sets her free.

* * *

IN MIYAZAKI's *Spirited Away*, we see this too. A witch has the power to make people forget their true natures by stealing their names. The protagonist helps free her friend, who sometimes takes the form of a boy and sometimes the form of a dragon, by figuring out his name. She tells him the story of how, when she was young, she fell into a river, and how it carried her to safety. She calls him by the river's name. His eyes grow wide. His silver scales shudder. He turns back into a boy. The naming is what does it. Saying it, speaking it aloud.

* * *

THROUGHOUT THIS PROCESS, I have learned many things' names, some of which I never wished to know. But in naming them, I can see them more clearly. Can pull them out of the fog.

Alcohol use disorder. Gaslighting. Devaluation. I know the names of you now.

Generalized anxiety. Panic disorder. Intergenerational trauma.

Codependency. Enabling. Fawning. I see now. I see your names.

I cannot fight what I cannot name. In naming, a pool. A mirror.

This truth is a kind of water magic. This truth is a sacred rain.

River

I study the lessons these characters offer. I try to move forward with grace.

* * *

About ten months after everything explodes, I am invited back to the desert state to read at a literary festival. I am excited, then nervous, then excited again. I want to return to the site of the scar. To go to the place where the wound was inflicted to see how far I have come.

The visit is a love bath. I am surprised to find that so many people want to see me and meet Cerulean, we barely have time to chat with them all in the short, three-day trip. Given that the narrative I had been fed often spoke of how friendless I was, this nudges my perception of this chapter of my life. Adjusting a tilted picture frame.

Near the end of the stay, I tell Cerulean I want to take him to the river. It runs along the edge of downtown, shaded by a canopy of trees. Bikers and joggers flow slowly by. The sun scatters light on the water.

We stand by a ring of stone benches where I used to sit with children as a part of a summer camp I taught at for years. There, we would paint with watercolors or listen to sounds in nature, taking a moment for stillness, for appreciation. Stones in a bustling stream.

Cerulean and I stand in silence. The river gushes by.

I think about the people we have visited on this trip. People who reflect the different communities I was part of. The nonprofit. The college. The writing groups. How their work tries to hold space, to lift people up. To encourage and empower. I think about them doing this work in a state that constantly slashes education budgets, passes repressive legislation. How they get up and do it anyway. Despite that constant opposition.

To do that work takes guts and faith. They have my limitless respect.

"It makes a difference," I say aloud. "That work. It makes a difference." If any would dare to devalue it, my response would be: *How dare you?*

Across many fantasy narratives, water magic mends wounds. It feels right to say this near a river.

* * *

LATER THAT DAY, we stop by a consignment store, and I find a dress in my size—only one—with a pattern of red birds emerging from cages.

"A symbol," I say, laughing. I purchase it at once. I wear it on our last day there.

I have described my heart as a red bird in poems. Have winced to Vanessa Carlton's song "Miner's Canary," which uses the title's metaphor to explore an unhealthy relationship, as I slowly recuperate my strength. Have thought about this image, the cruelty of it: keeping a bird underground.

Just before we leave for the airport, I snap a photo of myself. In it, my face looks joyful. Nothing like the "fake smile" the man of mist often accused me of wearing during my years in the desert state. On my shoulders and chest, the red birds fly free.

It feels elemental: the river, the fabric, our words bending airwaves as we speak. The experience feels alchemic, catalytic. A living, breathing spell.

Horror Vacui

Ekphrasis on *She-Ra and the Princesses of Power*, *The Myth of Demeter and Persephone*, and *Witch Heart*

The image that used to come to mind when I thought of love was a flower growing out of my chest. It took the form of a stargazer lily. It sat left-of-center, like a boutonniere, directly over my heart. The first time I saw it was in my twenties, the day I realized I was developing feelings for the man of mist. It appeared there spontaneously, blooming under my clavicle. Petals dusted with pollen and red spots. "You make me feel magenta and orange," I said. The flower: magenta and orange.

It may be worth mentioning that when I told him this, he responded, "I don't know what that means."

* * *

WHEN WE WERE MARRIED, there were many times when I felt saddened, or angered, or let down. Each time, my mind's eye conjured the flower being cut. I pictured its blossom being lopped off, the shocked green circle of stem. But also, each time, the flower grew back. Involuntarily. I would find myself full of empathy, compassion. The petals would reopen like fingers reaching out to mend whatever rip had been made.

This, I thought, was what would make the marriage work. This mystical, unbidden flower. Earned or not, forgiveness would well up. The impulse to repair.

Now, I understand, that impulse might have gone by many other names: fear of abandonment, overcompensation, denial, self-betrayal. But back then, it looked like love.

* * *

WHEN EVERYTHING EXPLODED, he spoke so coldly—so sharply—over days, a new image came. Not just cutting the flower. But pulling it up by the root. It tried to grow back. It kept trying to grow. But this image came, repeatedly: him yanking it out like a weed.

"I hope this won't need to be a *long* conversation," he said icily, when he confirmed he was done for good. No counseling. No waiting.

I get it. No warmth. No light.

My back against the wall of a public restroom stall, I told the flower, "Don't grow back, now." I stared at the patch where it had been, and told it, "Don't grow back."

* * *

A FRIEND WHO HAS been married a long, long time said, "You have what it takes to be married. I know you would have stuck it out." He sighed and stared at the table and continued, "It's just good you don't have to."

A shiver of recognition ran through me. All three statements felt true.

* * *

I WOULD HAVE STAYED. I would have stayed.

It is good I did not have to.

* * *

AFTER RECEIVING the job offer, after allowing myself to confess to Cerulean, I bring my things to my father's house. I sit in a lawn chair wearing oversized sunglasses, dazed, and watch him water his plants. The sun is incongruent with the chaos in my chest. He tries to keep the conversation light.

He points out the groundcover plant that weaves along the garden's edge, circumventing stepping-stones and baskets.

"It really went everywhere," he says, nodding at its leaves, its tiny blooms scattered like confetti. The blue star creeper filling gaps in, as if poured. "I guess nature really does abhor a vacuum."

* * *

ALL SUMMER, I ask myself: "Is it strong, or weak?" To keep my heart open, to act on what love was suppressed there. To break and build at once.

On our second day together in person, Cerulean and I eat lunch on a grassy hill that overlooks the ocean. We share a spoon. The pampas fronds billow. The sun does not feel incongruent.

A thought streaks through my mind like a comet-tailed star: *I am so happy, I think I might be dead.*

I literally search my memory for traces of my own demise. Because this would be heaven. Right here.

* * *

ONCE, WHEN I WAS YOUNGER, I spent the summer dancing in a portside cabaret. In a number set to "The Cellblock Tango" from *Chicago,* I was cast as the innocent one—the one who, in fact, was not guilty. I was to do a twirl, then fall backward into a troupe member's arms, land in a deep dip with my foot pointed upward, my long hair brushing the floor.

For weeks, I struggled to get it just right. I had little dancing experience.

The night of the show, I performed it perfectly. I felt the difference in my bones.

This was like that. My body took over. Instinct told me what to do.

* * *

WATCHING *She-Ra and the Princesses of Power,* ND Stevenson's reboot of the 1980s show, I felt a strong affection and affinity for the character of Perfuma. A princess who wields vines.

Perfuma tries to be serene, but she is a bit antsy. She meditates and grinds her teeth. Discussing what her weakness is, a friend tells her she stifles her potential out of fear of hurting those she loves.

Perfuma has a morning tea ritual. Perfuma's eyelid occasionally twitches.

But she makes flowers grow, green and abundant. She weaves blossoms into her hair.

* * *

IN PHYSICS, the idea of *horror vacui*—nature's abhorrence of vacuums—can be traced back to Aristotle. It shows up in art history, too, referring to highly ornate designs.

Véronique Plesch writes that although some critics perceive such art to be chaotic, even compulsive, others see it as an expression of an artist's limitless creativity. It simply can't be constrained.

What fills in the white space may not be random, but beautiful. Desired.

* * *

I STARE AT THE PATCH where the lily grew. I see a tiny shoot push through the soil.

Is it strong, or weak? I spy another tendril. I watch a wispy sprout unfurl.

* * *

IN *SHE-RA*, the only place Perfuma gets truly angry is in a sandy dune. She struggles with the cacti, their jagged spikes and spines. She is at her worst in the desert.

Only when she stops pleading with what sits above ground does she learn what she must. When she shifts her focus to the subterranean roots, her magical abilities succeed.

Sometimes it is in the unseen places that the most potent work is going on.

* * *

VISITING CERULEAN'S PARENTS for dinner one night, his mother gestures to a potted plant he brought home from work years ago.

"Look," she says. "It's flowering." She stares at us over her glasses. "It has never flowered before."

Strong, or weak? We hold hands under the table. A pair of entwining roots.

* * *

IN MY MIND, I EMBRACE my adolescent self. She was a child. She did not deserve those burdens, nor that blame. She did not deserve to punish herself for nearly twenty years, screaming her grief at the sky.

Through forgiveness, the floodgates are finally opened. What flows out is love, undistorted.

* * *

ALMOST A YEAR after everything explodes, my father comes to see me in my new home. He asks about some art he gave me, and whether I am going to put it up.

I know the art he means. It is boxed at the back of the closet. It is in the only box whose tape I still have yet to cut. He sent it to me when I was living in the desert state. It is a copy of eight etchings by Roberto Rascovich from 1903. *The Myth of Demeter and Persephone.*

One etching of Persephone hung in my old home. The rest had lived in storage. This and my anxiety around the story—that of a woman pulled underground—have kept me from wanting to see them. But it does seem unfair for the art to gather dust, and given all my thoughts of flowers and Perfuma, I feel open to a lesson from Persephone, a deity of springtime.

I open the box, and there at the front is the image that hung in my old home. I quickly flip past it, and there, to my shock, is an image of two goddesses, one of whom holds torches, one of whom points the way forward.

I flip the etching over. The text has been attached to the back of each frame, keeping the pictures and story paired.

"No one heard her cry except Hecate," it reads, "sitting in her cave thinking delicate thoughts, and the sun."

I have full-body shivers.

* * *

AROUND HALLOWEEN, Cerulean and I go to a goth shop I frequented as an undergrad. It has pendants and charms and candles and carvings—all kinds of enchanting things.

And art, of course. I flip through greeting cards. I come across one in luscious colors—bold and vibrant hues. It depicts a heart overflowing with flowers: foxglove, bluebells, poppies. At its base are curving, searching roots.

The artist, Laura Tempest Zakroff, titles the painting *Witch Heart*.

* * *

WEEKS EARLIER, I drafted a poem reflecting on the patch where the lily used to grow. How it must have looked like nothing could blossom there. How it must have looked like ruined earth.

But in its wake, a garden grew. Not just a new flower. A garden. All kinds of plants sprung up in me. Things I didn't know I could grow.

Jonquil laughs with family. Late-night jasmine chats with friends. Hyacinth discussions of readings with students. Lavender bus rides through the rain. The lilac stillness of my own company, gazing out the window drinking coffee.

And of course, the sky-blue flower, twisting toward the light. Open petals drinking the sun.

I grew all manner of various blooms. A witch's heart, full to the brim.

* * *

IN HER FAMOUS BOOK on feminine figures in myth and folk-lore, *Women Who Run With the Wolves*, Clarissa Pinkola Estés mentions Hecate only once. Estés writes that the goddess "has about her the smell of humus and the breath of God." This is in a chapter on emotional deserts, places where sustenance seems scarce.

But, Estés writes, there *is* life in the desert. She writes that it is just "very condensed." She gives the example of a cactus with one flower, pieced together from what moisture is there. So much goes into that flower.

I thought I was capable of just one thing: only regrowing that flower. And yes, I was condensed. And yes, it took effort. And yes, there is beauty in that.

But given the chance, I would rather be a garden. Lush with buzzing, with dew.

Lanterns
Ekphrasis on *Tangled*

A few weeks before everything explodes, for my birthday, my mother sends me a canvas print of an image inspired by the Disney movie *Tangled,* an adaptation of the fairy tale "Rapunzel." In it, Rapunzel and her love interest Flynn Rider sit in a gondola watching floating lanterns in the night sky. Rapunzel has been wondering what the lanterns are for her whole life, not knowing that they are offered each year in honor of the princess kidnapped as a baby, who turns out to be her. She stares dreamily up at the glowing display, having longed for this moment for years. Behind her, Flynn holds two lanterns. Knowing it has been her longtime wish, he prepared for the occasion and wants her to participate. It is a tender, romantic scene.

I loved the gift, but I was not sure where I would put it. Where in the world would I hang this piece of art the man of mist would surely roll his eyes at? It wasn't his thing. He indulged me once by watching it. But the movie was not to his taste.

Barely two weeks later, we would be separated. I would put the painting in a box.

* * *

DURING ONE OF THE many phone calls Cerulean and I had while I was staying with my mother, waiting to hear from the job, somehow, *Tangled* came up.

"Oh," he said. "I love that movie. Especially the scene with the lanterns."

My heart twinkles like champagne.

* * *

A DRESS I HAD ordered years ago got lost in a costume maker's pile of orders, then further delayed by the pandemic. As these things often go, it finally arrived in my year of enormous change. It was Rapunzel's dress. It came right before Halloween.

"I'll be Flynn Rider!" Cerulean said. He dashed to the closet and came out as Flynn. All of these items he had right on hand. Brown pants. White shirt. Green vest. The pants and shirt, granted, aren't that strange. But a green vest? Really? I beamed.

In a photo we take, according to a friend, we look like kindred spirits. The word that often comes to mind is "easy." Not easy in a way that would make me complacent. Not easy meaning perfect. But less like growing flowers through concrete.

It feels like a garden where things are meant to grow. With both of us tending the tilth.

* * *

THE PAINTING HANGS in the new home we build, with its walls that come the color of tea roses. Gently, gently, we tend its roots. Watch its petals faintly shine.

Open Heart Fruit

We are eating pistachios in our home one day, and Cerulean tells me the characters that make up the word for *pistachio* in Cantonese, 開心果, translate individually to *open heart fruit*. Together, those for *open* and *heart* also mean happiness.

He holds up one of the nuts, the green of it visible beneath its hard encasing. How it could so easily emerge from its shell with just a small nudge of the thumb.

"See?" he says. "I like to think it's called that because when it's ready, it shows its heart."

When it is ready, it shows its heart. Maybe this is an instruction in happiness.

Diorama

Ekphrasis on *Frozen*

The holidays come and I am invited to participate in a baking challenge by a friend. It is the second year of the challenge, and part of the task is to make a Bûche de Noël, a notoriously difficult French cake decorated to look like a Yule log. Last year, I had spent five hours sweating over the cake, eventually recruiting the man of mist to help. This year, I want to do it alone. I have better equipment this time, and experience. I am confident I can make it work.

One baker in the first challenge not only created a gorgeous caramel Bûche de Noël but added tiny figurines from *Star Wars* to make the cake the centerpiece in a diorama of the planet Endor. I was tickled by this. I resolved at the time to get more ambitious in round two. Now, that time had come.

My affection for *Frozen* had been a good-natured joke among friends, so I opted for decorations in line with that theme. *Winter cake, winter movie,* I thought. There was not much more to it than that.

But as I began to brainstorm the layout for the figurines I had bought, a host of emotions began to unfold. I felt indignation for Elsa, an introvert whom I perceived to be a bit overshadowed and pathologized in the film. I wanted her to be able to shine. I felt protective of her.

After frosting the cake to look like bark and gluing meringue mushrooms on with dots of melted chocolate, I placed Elsa front and center on the log. I wanted her to know I saw her. Valued her. This felt oddly necessary.

I realized, partially laughing at myself, but also deeply serious, my activity shared something in common with a technique my mother studied when I was young: an art therapy practice involving trays of sand. In sandtray therapy, participants arrange small toys in a box of sand and tell a story as they do so, with part of the idea being that this playful approach will allow the participant to address— and potentially begin to resolve—issues causing distress. As Karrie L. Swan and April A. Schottelkorb state in one study, some theorists believe this is because the mind can identify in the archetypal toys, heroes and villains both, reflections of its own struggles. What characters people feel drawn to, repelled by, angry toward, and so on can provide psycholog- ical insight. The sandtray becomes an arena where ideas can clash and get worked out. (So too, perhaps, in bibliotherapy; so too, perhaps, in ekphrasis.)

I sat Elsa on top of the cake and felt a sense of gravity and lightness all at once. It was playful and ridiculous. It was vital and symbolic. Her small face gazed upward, her hands outstretched to receive what the starlight had to bring.

Irreconcilable

During the long-ago visit to the desert state where I scrubbed mold off his wall, I had the man of mist's apartment to myself for a few hours while he was at work. In this time, I cut a heart out of red construction paper and taped it to his kitchen cupboard. When he came home and saw it, he smiled softly, but averted his eyes—looking sad, or maybe just uneasy. It was an expression I have never seen on another face since.

Bittersweet, maybe. Like he knew something I did not. Like he glimpsed through time and spied that this was the kind of dynamic that would make two people check the box for Irreconcilable Differences on a marriage's death certificate years hence.

Again, it's not that I didn't notice. I certainly saw it. I noticed. I just wanted to believe that determination and I could overcome anything. Even whatever it was that caused that enigmatic smile.

This man could be gregarious, witty, and observant. But also, it always felt like a part of him was drifting away into mist. Elusive. Guarded. Arching away. Even as I tried to lean in.

* * *

LATER, I WILL LEARN about attachment styles—anxious and avoidant—and think, *His teeth were a perfect fit for the indents of my wounds.*

* * *

"IT'S ALL RIGHT to acknowledge," my therapist says once, "that the dynamic held tragic aspects."

And though this is not a tragedy, yes, there are tragic aspects.

* * *

THE CLOSEST I EVER SAW to a repeat of that expression was when he and I visited my hometown after my third interview for the job. It was looking like I might get it at that point, and he wanted to explore prospective neighborhoods. As we ate dinner at a dimly lit brewery, I began telling him about some of the animated films I had watched, made by students at the school where I was applying.

He looked at me incredulously, and with something like annoyance. "You're crying," he said. I hadn't noticed, but I was. I found them that beautiful. I wanted the job that much.

Go, I can imagine him saying, arms crossed. *If you want it that badly, just go.*

* * *

BY BREAKING IT SO completely, he made the transition easier. I know this, and part of me is thankful.

Yet in some scenario in the vast multiverse, I wonder if we could have parted ways without so much pain. There need not have been so much anguish and repression.

In that universe, perhaps, there are just differences. Differences, irreconcilable.

The Forge
Ekphrasis on *Magic Knight Rayearth*

In the anime *Magic Knight Rayearth*, the heroes are bestowed with fragments of ore that evolve along with their hearts. The ore, which starts out as a gleaming chunk of rock, is smithed into armor that gradually shapeshifts as each girl grows stronger and braver. The armor does not come out of the ground fully formed. It has to grow. It has to evolve.

Having been through what I have, I see love like this. It comes in many metals. Some flimsy, like nickel. Easily bent. Some more solid, like gold. Or even stronger. Steel, iron, or diamond.

I want to polish love to its shiniest state. I want to hone a love that's dent-resistant. I am unafraid to hammer away on the anvil of myself. To forge the highest-quality love.

The Sacrament

As Ann Patchett writes in her essay "The Sacrament of Divorce," there is no widespread ritual marking the end of a marriage. But arguably, there should be. If weddings, births, and funerals are occasions for rituals, divorces should be too. It is an enormous life transition. At least, it has been for me.

If marriage means making a promise, divorce means at least one person admitting that the promise needs to be broken. Even if both people agree, it is still a heavy thing to bear. If a marriage begins with mutual hope—and I know, not all do, but at least some do—divorce means the surrender of that hope. That is something that deserves a ritual.

And as if navigating this terrain were not difficult enough already—emotionally, but then there is also the invasion of such an intimate part of life by seemingly endless bureaucracy—it is a transition with an implication of scarring, permanent shame. It is a word used in punchlines, cloaked in stigma. Look at the representations of people who have experienced divorce in popular media. Those I have seen have not been flattering. Nor very dignified. Nor realistic. The subtext seems to be—on and off screens—that this passage will inextricably mar you. Not just your past, but your future, too. Like you are handed a scarlet letter to wear, or handcuffed to a suitcase of rocks.

The implication seems, to me, to be that whatever genre your life was before, it must now be a tragedy or farce. And that feels grossly unfair.

I think I was at risk of this until I realized it is just one more example of a patriarchal narrative trying to silence people of all genders who have been through something difficult. In my own life, I have been discouraged from talking about everything from ordinary processes like menstruation to traumas like sexual assault. I thought of the courage I admired in others who broke the silence around these and other frequently silenced things. I thought of people who spoke up because they knew that shame can feast on silence and that silence can bring with it countless kinds of pain.

"Divorce" is a word that still feels dirty on my tongue. It is an ugly word; it was probably designed to be. One more reason to keep it locked up. But it does not *have* to be a dirty word. As Patchett writes, it can be liberatory. It can signify a fresh start in life.

I resent the implication that a person's life, following a divorce, is some kind of sad epilogue to their "true" story. Rather, it is just one chapter in their book. There are many chapters left to write.

The genre of your life can be whatever you want, even after a difficult life event like this. It can still be an adventure, a romance, a comedy. You are still you. Your story can keep going.

It would be easier to make this transition, I think—in its pain and possibility both—if there were some tools to mark the occasion. But there is no white veil, there is no tuxedo. No christening gown, no coffin. At least in the culture I grew up in, we are on our own in this one.

Writing this has been one attempt at a ritual. A thousand tiny rituals. I have cobbled together one method of healing. Looked for my own broken branches, circles of indented grass, as I have tracked hope through the winding forest of myself and come out the other side.

* * *

A FRIEND ASKS, "What do you do with that time? The time spent alive in the coffin?" The Sleeping Beauty time, time spent in hibernation, while trauma responses circle the stone-gray castle with breath made of fire. *What do we do with the time spent in survival mode?* is what I think he is asking.

And I don't know, entirely. I cannot erase it. All I can do is try to learn from it. All I can do is sift through the fragments and try to find gold in the silt. To recommit to my own happiness, more ardently than ever before. To commit to polishing love to a shine, to make love the sun at the center of my life.

* * *

KATE ZAMBRENO WARNS against turning people in our lives into stock characters in our stories. And I don't want to succumb to that. There are no cartoon villains here. The man of mist, and even the beast, are complex. Every person is more than an archetype. I can sit with the contradictions.

* * *

IN FACT, I want to tell you a story: when I admitted I was way in over my head with the first Bûche de Noël, I implored the man of mist to help, and he did. At one point, I looked down and found my pants covered in powdered sugar from the thighs all the way to the toes. We laughed about that, belly-laughed, standing in the home we shared.

What to do with this memory? Knowing we were both so limited, so fallible? Knowing that despite some good faith efforts, we both had our eyes on the exit? That in just a few months, we would never speak again? How do you categorize it?

I suppose, despite everything, I am grateful for this moment. And the time we ate waffles under the moon, surrounded by crickets and frog song. And the time we drank wine from a thermos in the park, watched the sunset over a hill.

I'm not suggesting this approach would be right for everyone, or in every case. But for me, there's some measure of peace to be found in this. These small snapshots, I would not wish away. I think my heart is richer for them.

*   *   *

WHEN WE WERE TRYING to make that Bûche de Noël, something wasn't working with the eggs. We had no electric mixer, so we took turns whisking the egg whites in a bowl by hand. They were not gelling. They would not turn to meringue. I would later learn this method was absurd, that a mixer is an obvious must. But I was new at this. I did not know. I did not know what I lacked.

I was lamenting the loss of six free-range eggs, not wanting for them to be wasted. After scouring the internet for meringue-saving tips, I came across a buried post in a forum that suggested taking another, new egg and whisking its white separately. Turning *that* one into meringue-consistency, then adding it to the failed egg bowl had a chance of sparing the whole batch, the post claimed.

We tried it. The new egg thickened. We poured it in the failed bowl. And lo and behold, when we began whisking, the rest of the eggs followed suit. The Bûche de Noël was saved.

When we sat eating slices of the log cake later, after photographing it by the Christmas tree, I said, "I never thought that egg trick would actually work."

"Really?" he answered. "I didn't either. I only agreed to try it because I thought you wanted to. I didn't want to let you down."

Surprised, I said, "The only reason I tried it at all was because I thought *you* thought it would work. I was ready to throw the whole thing away."

We laughed about this. How our doubts came second to something like hope, and how something good came of it. How something we both privately deemed impossible somehow catalyzed and worked.

It worked until it didn't. Some things are fleeting. Sometimes, that is not a bad thing.

There are truths we will never know about each other. Aspects we will never understand.

*　*　*

MAYBE SOME MARRIAGES are mercurial, alchemical. Nudged along by forces human eyes can never see. Sugar and salt often look indiscernible—we might not know the difference until it's in our mouth. Until it is inside of us.

Maybe some marriages' ends are like this too: chemical reactions, unseen bonds, slowly unfolding, unfurling.

*　*　*

AT THE BOTTOM of the Hecate candle were chunks of snowflake obsidian. I look up its meaning. *Balance,* I read. The duality.

Salt and sugar both.

The Moon Made Full

My birthday comes, and Cerulean and I go to a water-themed exhibit at the local art museum. It gathers art from all over the world and all throughout time. It examines water as life-giving and life-taking, fragile and mysterious and strong. Inadvertently, I wear a blue silk top I had not worn since my first interview for the job. A garment, I suppose, that represented courage. Moving toward happiness.

The anniversary comes of the day when everything exploded, the week where everything changed. I consider going to the local Locks, one of the last places the man of mist and I visited together on the trip where we were supposedly scoping out potential neighborhoods. At the Locks, ships pass between fresh water and salt water. The transition takes them some time.

Boats that want to travel from the freshwater lake to the salt water of the sound must get locked up in a concrete box. The water level lowers, and it must feel like they are sinking. But then the gates open, and they sail out to sea. The ocean so much wilder, so much vaster than the lake. Uncertainty, but fresh breezes, too.

The day everything changed, there was a new moon in the sky. A year later, what astronomers are calling a Super Flower Blood Moon Eclipse sits in the air. Glowing like a gentle flame.

In the end, I do not end up going to the Locks. The day of the full moon, Cerulean and I paint a wall in our home the color of a cloudless sky.

* * *

WHEN HE HEARD I was applying for a job back home—months before everything exploded—Cerulean bought me a cookbook he liked. He told me it would have been a house-warming present. A friendly congratulations gift.

Now, in the kitchen we share, we flip through pages. Together, we cook a soup from it instead.

Author's Note

The stories, characters, and images I've written about here are ones that helped offer healing for me as I navigated a very challenging year. There is much more to say about all of them. I've done my best to write about these narratives with humility, care, and respect—with appreciation and admiration, never appropriation. That said, I know that my reflections are inevitably shaped by my own privileges, experiences, and limitations. If this work has been insensitive in any way, I sincerely apologize, and I will do my best to listen, learn, grow, and do better in the future.

It is essential to hear from many different voices as we continue to examine representation, storytelling, and healing. My hope is that this book will be just one small contribution to that much larger conversation.

Thank you very much to Writing Diversely for their sensitivity read, which helped guide the book.

* * *

The book was primarily written between May 2021 and May 2022, with a few revisions and additions made after that. While there is much art I have encountered since the summer of 2022 that I could certainly comment on in ways pertinent to *Water Spell*—the *Ahsoka* episode where Ahsoka sees flashes of Anakin and Darth Vader simultaneously, Storm's epic defeat of The Adversary in *X-Men '97*, Primrose's journey in *Octopath Traveler*, representations of anxiety in *Inside Out 2*, and more—I decided to limit my reflections to media I saw in and prior to the year when the book was drafted. This means that continuations of characters' stories that came out after mid-2022, such as Wanda's and Shinobu's, are not taken into account. The scope of the book had to end somewhere, and while much could be said about newer media, I wanted to do my best to maintain the writing in the form it came to me: a yearlong narrative and ritual.

* * *

The book brings up some difficult topics, including alcohol use disorder and sexual assault. For a list of resources that may be able to help with these and other painful experiences, please visit www.apa.org/topics/crisis-hotlines. No one should have to face a crisis alone.

* * *

The book reflects my impressions and memories of the past. Dialogue is not meant to be word-for-word transcription.

* * *

My goal has always been to write in the spirit of healing, never harm. I hope that the telling of this story offers something positive to others.

Acknowledgments

Thank you to Shilo, fairy godmother of this book, who gently held the first few fragments I eked out while still in the thick of it all and saw them for what they were: the start of a larger, longer project. Thank you for not asking my story to be more linear, less figurative, or anything other than what it needed to be, especially in those early stages. It is because of you that I came to the lyric essay as a form in the first place, and I continue to learn from and admire your work.

Thank you to Jason, mystic godfather of this book, who has believed in it from the start. There were many times when I experienced doubt and fear along the way, and your encouragement always helped get me back on my feet.

Thank you to my family, not only for helping to see me through the events described in the book, but for ushering me into lifelong conversations about the value and beauty of the arts. Mom, Dad, Will, Ember, Dave, BriAnne, Sarah, Susie: thank you. Thank you to my mom, especially, for seeing the spirit of the book and having faith in it, and in me.

Thank you to the many other loved ones who helped support and guide the book too, both during the summer of 2021 and the years that have passed since. In particular, thank you to Hannah, Wendy, Lisa, Lessie, Jenn, Jenny, Betsy, Cristina, Stefanie, Kyle, Ryan, Tess, Mical, Rachel, May, Nazia, Lila,

Katie, Courtney, Amber, Danielle, Remy, Megan, Hillary, Kim, Bryn, and Ray for your friendship. Thank you to the fellow teachers and writing group friends, especially Laura, Lynne, Carl, Ryan, Alisa, and Jana, who were among the first readers of several fragments. Thank you to my beloved new family members, too, for making me feel so welcome.

In addition, thank you to Claire, Sonia, and Fara for mentorship and guidance during my first year back in my home state, and since. Special thanks to Kari for very insightful feedback on the Shinobu and Wanda pieces. Thank you to Mardi for believing in the best in me during a turbulent time, and for never batting a lash when I asked yet again if I could compare what I was going through to a piece of pop culture. Thank you to Julie for encouragement and support during the book's final edits and release. Thank you to Annabel for assistance with quote permissions requests. To each and every other person who offered a kind word during this transition in my life, thank you.

Thank you to all the artists out there working to make the world a better place. Your work inspires me.

Thank you to Cornerstone Press for seeing something of value in the book, and for guiding it to publication. My thanks extend to the whole team, especially Dr. Ross Tangedal and Ellie Atkinson.

And, of course, thank you to "Cerulean" for finding me in a high school anime club in the year 2000 and being part of my life ever since. Thank you for our past. Thank you for our future. Thank you for showing me such love.

* * *

Gratitude is also extended to the following creators and organizations:

Thank you to the editors of *Luna Luna Magazine*, where "Trouble" first appeared in an earlier form.

Thank you to the editors of *Superstition Review*, where "Haunted Mall" first appeared in an earlier form.

The quoted portion of "Becoming the Labyrinth: Negotiating Magical Space and Identity in *Puella Magi Madoka Magica*" by Sara Cleto and Erin Kathleen Bahl appears courtesy of the authors.

The quoted portion of *Speak: The Graphic Novel* appears courtesy of Farrar, Straus and Giroux BYR.

The quoted portion of *The Wheel of Time:* "The Dragon Reborn" appears courtesy of Sony Pictures Television/Amazon.

The quoted portion of *The Myth of Demeter and Persephone* by Roberto Rascovich is in the public domain, via the Smithsonian American Art Museum.

The quoted portion of *Women Who Run With the Wolves* by Clarissa Pinkola Estés appears courtesy of Penguin Random House LLC.

Thank you to all those involved in the creation of these works.

Bibliography

Ahsoka. Created by Dave Filoni. Lucasfilm, 2023.

Amélie. Directed by Jean-Pierre Jeunet. Miramax, 2001.

Anderson, Laurie Halse. *Speak*. Kindle ed., Farrar, Straus and Giroux, 1999.

---. *Speak: The Graphic Novel*. Illustrated by Emily Carroll, Farrar, Straus and Giroux, 2018.

Aristotle. *Poetics*. Translated by S. H. Butcher. Project Gutenberg, 2008, https://www.gutenberg.org/files/1974/1974-h/1974-h.htm.

Avatar: The Last Airbender. Created by Michael Dante DiMartino and Bryan Konietzko. Nickelodeon Animation Studios, 2005.

Aye, Jacque. *Adorned by Chi*. Illustrated by Magus Ato, cover artist, Tiana Mone'e, Adorned by Chi LLC, 2018.

"Banned and Challenged Picture Books." Edmonton Public Library, Feb. 2018, https://epl.bibliocommons.com/list/share/69128707/70680896?page=3.

Beaumont, Jeanne-Marie LePrince de. "Beauty and the Beast." 15 November 2011, https://sites.pitt.edu/~dash/beauty.html.

Blanc, Lola. "Angry Too." Duetti, 2019.

Brown, Adrienne Maree. "The Power in Pleasure." *YES!*, YES! Media, 18 May 2022, https://www.yesmagazine.org/issue/pleasure/2022/05/18/power-in-pleasure-adrienne-maree-brown.

Captain Marvel. Directed by Anna Boden and Ryan Fleck, Marvel Studios, 2019.

Carlton, Vanessa. "Miner's Canary." *Love is an Art*, Dine Alone Music Inc., 2020.

Carroll, Emily. Interview by ROOM. "An interview with Emily Carroll: A Fairy-Tale Teller in the Digital Age." *ROOM Magazine*, vol. 37, no. 3, https://roommagazine.com/an-interview-with-emily-carroll-a-fairy-tale-teller-in-the-digital-age/.

---. *Through the Woods.* Margaret K. McElderry Books, 2014.

Carter, Angela. *The Bloody Chamber.* Penguin Classics, 2015.

Cartwright, Mark. "Hecate." *World History Encyclopedia*, 22 Jun 2017, https://www.worldhistory.org/Hecate/.

CLAMP. *Tsubasa: Reservoir Chronicle.* Del Rey, 2004.

Cleto, Sara and Erin Kathleen Bahl. "Becoming the Labyrinth: Negotiating Magical Space and Identity in *Puella Magi Madoka Magica*." *Humanities*, vol. 5, no. 20, 2016, doi: 10.3390/h5020020.

Corn, Alfred. "Notes on Ekphrasis." *Poets.org*, Academy of American Poets, 2008, https://poets.org/text/notes-ekphrasis.

Crane, Walter. *The Blue Beard Picture Book.* John Lane, the Bodley Head, 1899, https://doi.org/10.5479/sil.450195.39088007530520.

Crash Landing on You. Created by Park Ji-eun, directed by Lee Jung-hyo. Netflix, 2019.

Crystal, Ana. "Snowflake Obsidian: Meaning, Healing Properties and Powers." *My Crystals*, 2021, https://www.mycrystals.com/meaning/snowflake-obsidian-meaning-healing-properties-and-powers.

Demon Slayer: Kimetsu no Yaiba. Created by Koyoharu Gotouge, directed by Haruo Sotozaki, Ufotable, 2019.

Demon Slayer: Kimetsu no Yaiba – The Movie: Mugen Train. Directed by Haruo Sotozaki, Ufotable, 2020.

Ellis, Bill. "The Fairy-telling Craft of *Princess Tutu*: Metacommentary and the Folkloresque." *The Folkloresque: Reframing Folklore in a Popular Culture World*, edited by Michael Dylan Foster and Jeffrey A. Tolbert, Utah State University Press, 2016, pp. 221-40.

Encanto. Directed by Jared Bush and Byron Howard. Walt Disney Animation Studios, 2021.

Estés, Clarissa Pinkola. *Women Who Run With the Wolves: Myths and Stories of the Wild Woman Archetype.* Ballantine Books, 1996.

Final Fantasy X. Square, 2001.

Frozen. Directed by Chris Buck and Jennifer Lee. Walt Disney Animation Studios, 2013.

Fruits Basket. Created by Natsuki Takaya, directed by Akitaro Daichi, Studio Deen, 2001.

Game of Thrones. Created by George R. R. Martin, directed by Benioff and D.B. Weiss, HBO Entertainment, 2011.

Gay, Ross. *The Book of Delights.* Algonquin Books, 2019.

Gay, Roxane. "What We Hunger For." *The Rumpus*, 12 April 2012, https://therumpus.net/2012/04/12/what-we-hunger-for/.

Glenum, Lara and Arielle Greenberg, editors. *Gurlesque: The New Grrly, Grotesque, Burlesque Poetics*. Saturnalia Books, 2010.

Gorman, Amanda. "The Hill We Climb." *YouTube*, uploaded by ABC News, 20 Jan. 2021, https://www.youtube.com/watch?v=Wz4YuEvJ3y4.

Graham, Ruth. "Against YA." *Slate*, The Slate Group, 5 June 2014, https://slate.com/culture/2014/06/against-ya-adults-should-be-embarrassed-to-read-childrens-books.html.

Gris. Nomada Studio, 2018.

Halberstam, Jack. *The Queer Art of Failure*. Duke University Press, 2011.

"Hide the Pain Harold." *Know Your Meme*, 2011, https://knowyourmeme.com/memes/hide-the-pain-harold.

Howl's Moving Castle. Directed by Hayao Miyazaki, Studio Ghibli, 2004.

Inside Out. Directed by Pete Docter, Pixar, 2015.

Inside Out 2. Directed by Kelsey Mann, Pixar, 2024.

Johnson, Jeffery C. "The Vale of Soul-Making." *The Paris Review*, 25 July 2014, https://www.theparisreview.org/blog/2014/07/25/the-vale-of-soul-making/.

Jones, Norah. "Good Morning." *Little Broken Hearts*, Blue Note Records, 2012.

Keats, John. "Selections from Keats's Letters." *Poetry Foundation*, 13 Oct. 2009, https://www.poetryfoundation.org/articles/69384/selections-from-keatss-letters.

Kittinette. "Shinobu Kocho | Angry Too." *YouTube*, 7 December 2021, https://www.youtube.com/watch?v=DSqMJGIHn2U.

Kingdom Hearts. Square Enix, 2002.

Kirszner, Laurie G. and Stephen R. Mandell. *Compact Literature*. Cengage, 2017.

Kübler-Ross, Elisabeth. *On Death and Dying: What the Dying Have to Teach Doctors, Nurses, Clergy and Their Own Families*. Scribner, 2014.

Lakoff, George and Mark Johnson. *Metaphors We Live By*. University of Chicago Press, 1980.

Lanyon, Charley. "Everyone Thought Flaming June Was Worthless, Now It's One of the World's Most Famous Paintings." *The Vindicated*, Vox Media, 2016, https://nymag.com/vindicated/2016/11/flaming-june-a-masterpiece-once-thought-worthless.html.

Lawless, Seph. "A Haunting Look Inside America's Creepiest Abandoned Malls." *Seph Lawless*, 2016, https://sephlawless.com/inside-creepiest-abandoned-malls/.

Leighton, Frederic. *Flaming June*. 1895.

Machado, Carmen Maria. "The Trash Heap Has Spoken." *Guernica*, 13 February 2017, https://www.guernicamag.com/the-trash-heap-has-spoken/.

Magic Knight Rayearth. Created by CLAMP, directed by Toshihiro Hirano, Yomiuri TV and Tokyo Movie Shinsha, 1995.

McCloud, Scott. *Understanding Comics: The Invisible Art*. HarperCollins, 1993.

Moana. Directed by John Musker and Ron Clements. Walt Disney Animation Studios, 2016.

Munsch, Robert. *The Paper Bag Princess*. Illustrated by Michael Martchenko, Annick Press, 2018.

National Oceanic and Atmospheric Administration. "Why Don't Satellites Fall Out of the Sky?" *National*

Environmental Satellite, Data, and Information Service, 27 Sept. 2017, https://www.nesdis.noaa.gov/news/ why-dont-satellites-fall-out-of-the-sky.

Octopath Traveler. Square Enix, 2018.

Odell, Jenny. *How To Do Nothing: Resisting the Attention Economy*. Melville House, 2019.

Patchett, Ann. *This is the Story of a Happy Marriage*. Harper Perennial, 2014.

Perrault, Charles. "The Story of Blue Beard." https:// americanliterature.com/author/charles-perrault/ fairy-tale/the-story-of-blue-beard.

Perry, Katy. "Electric." *YouTube*, 13 May 2021, https://www. youtube.com/watch?v=ojpTpT5i-PI.

"Pharrell Williams on Juxtaposition and Seeing Sounds." *NPR*, 13 December 2013, www.npr. org/sections/therecord/2013/12/31/258406317/ pharrell-williams-on-juxtaposition-and-seeing-sounds.

Plesch, Véronique. "When More is Better: Horror Vacui in History." *Maine Arts Journal*, 2021, https:// maineartsjournal.com/veronique-plesch-when-more-is-better-horror-vacui-in-history/.

Pokémon. Directed by Kunihiko Yuyama et al. OLM, Inc., 1997.

Prokofiev, Sergei. *Peter and the Wolf*. 1936.

"Quail." *Dream Encyclopedia*, 2020, https://www. dreamencyclopedia.net/quail.

Rascovich, Roberto. *The Myth of Demeter and Persephone*. 1903.

Revolutionary Girl Utena. Created by Be-Papas, directed by Kunihiko Ikuhara, TV Tokyo, 1997.

Rilke, Rainier Maria. "Archaic Torso of Apollo." Translated by Stephen Mitchell, *Poets.org*, Academy of American Poets, 1995, https://poets.org/poem/archaic-torso-apollo.

Sailor Moon. Created by Naoko Takeuchi, directed by Junichi Sato, Kunihiko Ikuhara, and Takuya Igarashi, Toei Animation, 1992.

screenocean. "Stevie Wonder Talks About Visualising Instruments (Ear Say '84)." *YouTube*, 6 July 2012, www.youtube.com/watch?v=TVG0cEJCZm8.

Simner, Julia. Interview by Kim I. Mills. "Speaking of Psychology: Tasty Words, Colorful Sounds: How People with Synesthesia Experience the World, with Julia Simner, PhD." *Speaking of Psychology*, episode 151, American Psychological Association, July 2021, https://www.apa.org/news/podcasts/speaking-of-psychology/synesthesia.

Smale, Holly [@HolSmale]. "Finally, the way we process emotions can vary. I have synaesthesia, so I often read emotions as colours. Trying to work out what 'dark purple' means can take time. In short, 'autistics can't read emotions' is overly simplistic and unhelpful. We can. Just not like you." *X*, 6 June 2021, https://x.com/HolSmale/status/1401522422273150986.

Sparks, Amber. "New Genres: Domestic Fabulism or Kansas with a Difference." *Electric Lit*, 26 June 2014, https://electricliterature.com/new-genres-domestic-fabulism-or-kansas-with-a-difference/.

Spirited Away. Directed by Hayao Miyazaki, Studio Ghibli, 2001.

Star Wars. Directed by George Lucas. Twentieth Century Fox, 1977.

Stevenson, ND. *She-Ra and the Princesses of Power*. DreamWorks Animation Television, 2018.

Stuller, Jennifer K. *Ink-stained Amazons and Cinematic Warriors: Superwomen in Modern Mythology*. Kindle ed., I.B. Tauris, 2010.

Styles, Harry. "Golden." *Fine Line*, Erskine Records Limited, 2019.

Swan, Karrie L. and April A. Schottelkorb. "Interpreting Children's Dreams Through Humanistic Sandtray Therapy." *International Journal of Play Therapy*, vol. 22, no. 3, 2013, pp. 119-128, https://www.apa.org/pubs/journals/features/pla-a0033389.pdf.

Tangled. Directed by Nathan Greno and Byron Howard. Walt Disney Animation Studios, 2010.

Teen Titans. Created by Bob Haney and Bruno Premiani, developed by Glen Murakami, David Slack, and Sam Register, Warner Bros., 2003.

Thrasher, Tyler. "Experiments // Crystallized." *Tyler Thrasher*, 2020, https://tylerthrasher.com/crystallized.

Tolstoy, Leo. *Anna Karenina*. Translated by Constance Garnett. Project Gutenberg, 1998, https://www.gutenberg.org/files/1399/1399-h/1399-h.htm.

The Tonight Show Starring Jimmy Fallon. "Billie Eilish Talks Happier Than Ever, Directing Music Videos and Her Synesthesia | the Tonight Show." *YouTube*, 10 Aug. 2021, www.youtube.com/watch?v=bRfgF_tXsGE.

Trites, Roberta Seelinger. *Disturbing the Universe: Power and Repression in Adolescent Literature*. University of Iowa Press, 2000.

WandaVision. Created by Jac Schaeffer, directed by Matt Shakman, Marvel Studios, 2021.

Watkins, Claire Vaye. "On Pandering." *Tin House*, 25 November 2015, https://tinhouse.com/on-pandering/.

Weiner, Jonah. "The Return of Lorde." *The New York Times Magazine*, The New York Times Company, 12 April 2017, https://www.nytimes.com/2017/04/12/magazine/the-return-of-lorde.html.

The Wheel of Time. Created by Robert Jordan, developed by Rafe Judkins, Sony Pictures Television and Amazon Studios, 2021.

White, Katie. "'Flaming June' Once Vanished for Decades—and Three Other Unexpected Facts About the Fiery Pre-Raphaelite Masterpiece." *Artnet*, 5 Oct. 2022, https://news.artnet.com/art-world/three-things-to-know-flaming-june-2170614.

X-Men. Created by Jack Kirby and Stan Lee, directed by Brian Singer. Marvel Studios, 2000.

X-Men '97. Created by Beau DeMayo, Marvel, 2024.

Yoshitani, Yoshi. *Tarot of the Divine: A Deck and Guidebook Inspired by Deities, Folklore, and Fairy Tales from Around the World*. Clarkson Potter, 2020.

Zakroff, Laura Tempest. *Witch Heart*. 2016.

Zambreno, Kate. *Heroines*. Semiotext(e), 2012.

Zeta-Jones, Catherine et al. "Cell Block Tango." *Chicago – Music from the Miramax Motion Picture*, Sony Music Entertainment, 2002.

Zimmer, Carl. "Many People Have a Vivid 'Mind's Eye,' While Others Have None at All." *The New York Times*, 8 June 2021, https://www.nytimes.com/2021/06/08/science/minds-eye-mental-pictures-psychology.html.

CATHERINE BROADWALL is the author of *Fulgurite* (Cornerstone Press, 2023), *Shelter in Place* (Spuyten Duyvil, 2019), and other collections. Her writing has appeared in *Bellingham Review, Colorado Review, Mid-American Review,* and other journals. She was the winner of the 2023 Paula Svonkin Creative Arts Award and the 2020 COG Poetry Award, as well as a finalist for the poetry categories of the 2021 Mississippi Review Prize and 2021 Pinch Literary Awards. Her website is www.catherinebroadwall.com.